DAY HIKES IN
YOSEMITE
NATIONAL PARK

55 GREAT HIKES

by Robert Stone

Day Hike Books, Inc.
RED LODGE, MONTANA

Published by Day Hike Books, Inc.
P.O. Box 865
Red Lodge, Montana 59068

Distributed by The Globe Pequot Press
246 Goose Lane
P.O. Box 480
Guilford, CT 06437-0480
800-243-0495 (direct order) · 800-820-2329 (fax order)
www.globe-pequot.com

Photographs by Robert Stone
Design by Paula Doherty

The author has made every attempt to provide accurate information in this book. However, trail routes and features may change—please use common sense and forethought, and be mindful of your own capabilities. Let this book guide you, but be aware that each hiker assumes responsibility for their own safety. The author and publisher do not assume any responsibility for loss, damage or injury caused through the use of this book.

Cover photo: Tuolumne River and the Cathedral Range
from Glen Aulin Trail, Hike 5.
Back cover photo: Taft Point, Hike 43.

Table of Contents

THE HIKES
Tioga Road

Tioga Road
Tuolumne Meadows Area

Tioga Road
West of Tuolumne Meadows

Hetch Hetchy to Big Oak Flat

Big Oak Flat Road and Foresta

Yosemite Valley

Glacier Point Road

Wawona and Mariposa Grove

About the Hikes

Yosemite National Park lies in central California on the western slope of the Sierra Nevada. The park's dramatic topography was sculpted by glaciers 10,000 years ago. The elevations range from 2,000 feet to 13,000-foot peaks along the eastern boundary. Although the park has 196 miles of roads, more than 90 percent of Yosemite is roadless wilderness with more than 750 miles of trails.

This guide includes 55 great hikes within this most scenic national park. The hikes have been chosen for their picturesque scenery, geological features, diversity and ability to be hiked within the day. Hikes range from easy to strenuous, accommodating all levels of experience. Highlights along the miles of hiking trails include incredible waterfalls, granite monoliths, expansive alpine meadows and unforgettable views from unique perspectives that are only available from the trails. To help you decide which hikes are most appealing to you, a brief summary of the highlights is included with each hike, along with a quick overview of distance, time and elevation gain. You may enjoy these areas for a short time or the whole day.

Yosemite's crown jewel is Yosemite Valley, a picturesque, seven-mile gorge chiseled by giant glaciers, which continues to be carved by the Merced River. The valley is home to 3,000-foot walls of granite massifs, smooth domes and an abundance of spectacular waterfalls leaping over tall, steep cliffs. Granite monoliths include Half Dome and El Capitan, rising 3,590 feet (over a half mile) above the valley. The valley's best-known waterfall is Yosemite Falls, which drops 2,425 feet. It is the highest falls in North America and fifth highest in the world. Hikes 30—37 explore this magnificent valley. Hikes range from easy paths along the Merced River valley to heart-pounding climbs up the granite cliffs.

To the north of the valley is Tuolumne Meadows and Tioga Pass, accessed by Tioga Road. Tioga Road is the highest paved auto route in California, crossing Tioga Pass at 9,945 feet. Hikes 1—21 lie along this road and explore the mid- to upper regions of the park, characterized by rugged alpine peaks and cobalt blue lakes. Hikes 12—13 and 15—16 allow the unique opportunity to see Yosemite Valley from its "back" side.

Tuolumne Meadows is the most often visited area along Tioga Road. The region here was formed by an enormous glacier 60 miles long and 2,000 feet thick. It carved out the largest subalpine meadow in the Sierra Nevada—Tuolumne Meadows. The meadow measures 2.5 miles long by a half mile wide and sits at an elevation of 8,600 feet. The glacier also formed polished granite domes, alpine lakes and deep canyons.

The meadow area is drained by tributaries of the Tuolumne River, which carves a winding path through the northern mountain terrain. The Hetch Hetchy Reservoir pools the river in a high, beautiful valley. Hikes 22—24 explore this area.

South of Yosemite Valley is Glacier Point Road, Hikes 38—49. Trails from this road offer easy access to Yosemite Valley's south rim. Paths lead to vistas atop 3,000-foot cliffs and some of the park's best panoramic vistas. The road also offers access to quiet forest strolls, a welcome respite from the crowds.

Farther south is the Wawona basin and meadow, home to the historic Wawona Hotel and a history museum. Hikes 50—53 are beautiful forest hikes along the South Fork Merced River and its tributaries.

Three giant sequoia groves are also found within the park—Mariposa Grove (Hikes 54—55), Merced Grove (Hike 27) and Tuolumne Grove (Hike 21). These small but impressive groves of towering trees complement the grandeur of the park's many awe-inspiring sights.

A few basic necessities will make your hike safer and more enjoyable. Wear supportive, comfortable hiking shoes. Bring hats, sunscreen, drinking water, snacks and appropriate outerwear. The weather can change quickly at these elevations. Stay on the trails and be aware of your own capabilities.

These hikes include some of the best scenery in Yosemite. Your time on the trails will undoubtedly add to your appreciation of this incredible park. Enjoy your hike!

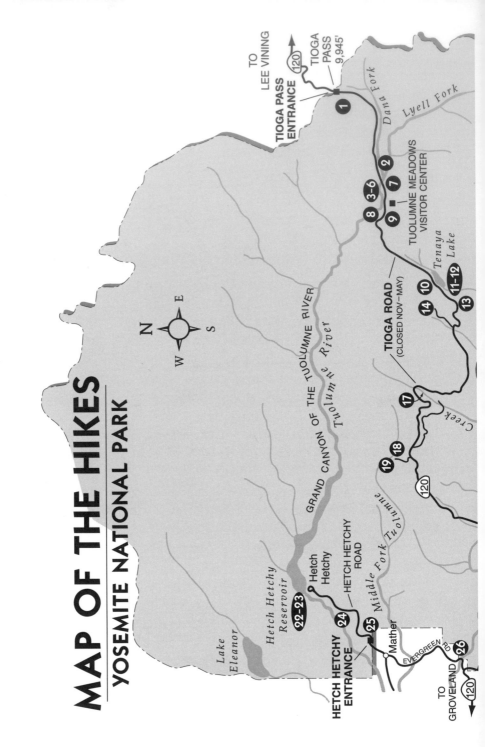

MAP OF THE HIKES
YOSEMITE NATIONAL PARK

TO LEE VINING

TIOGA PASS ENTRANCE

120

TIOGA PASS 9,945'

1

Dana Fork

Lyell Fork

2

3-6 **7**

8 **9**

TUOLUMNE MEADOWS VISITOR CENTER

Tenaya Lake

11-12

10 **13**

14

TIOGA ROAD (CLOSED NOV–MAY)

N E S W

GRAND CANYON OF THE TUOLUMNE RIVER

Tuolumne River

17

Creek

18

19

120

Middle Fork Tuolumne

Hetch Hetchy Reservoir

Hetch Hetchy

HETCH HETCHY ROAD

22-23

24

25

HETCH HETCHY ENTRANCE

Mather

EVERGREEN RD.

26

Lake Eleanor

TO GROVELAND

120

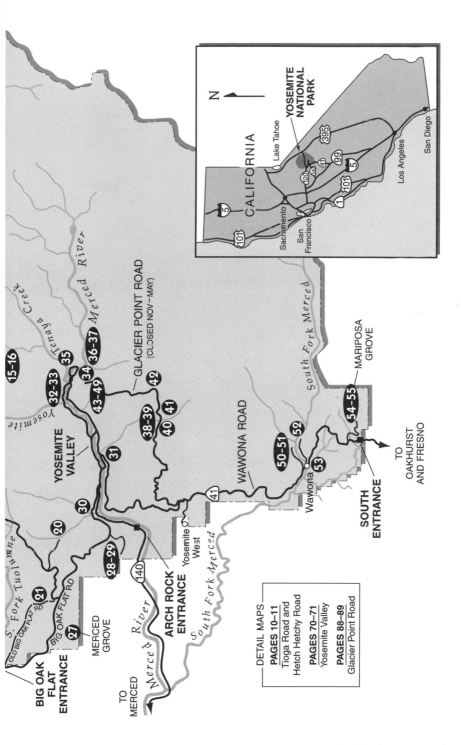

DETAIL MAPS
PAGES 10–11
Tioga Road and
Hetch Hetchy Road

PAGES 70–71
Yosemite Valley

PAGES 88–89
Glacier Point Road

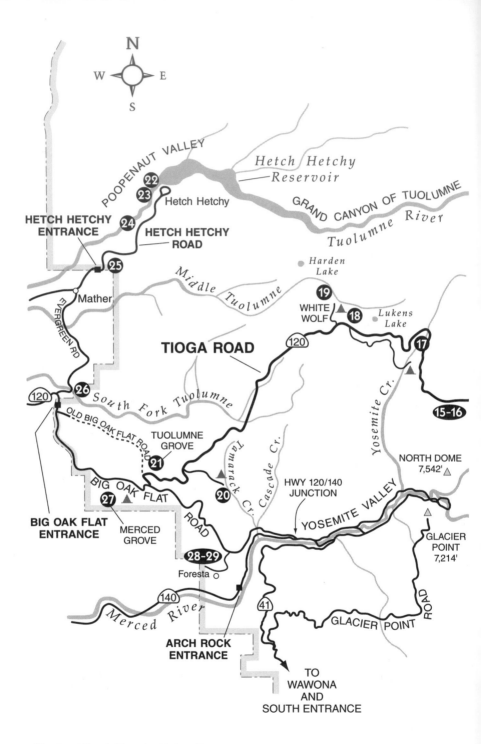

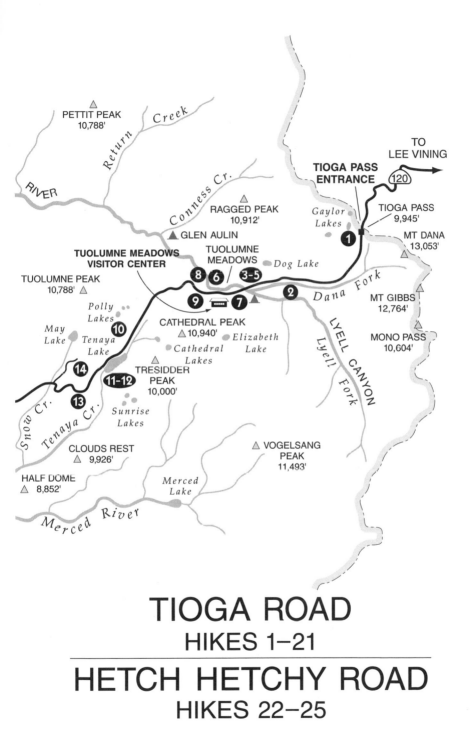

TIOGA ROAD
HIKES 1–21

HETCH HETCHY ROAD
HIKES 22–25

Hike 1
Middle and Upper Gaylor Lakes

Hiking distance: 4 miles round trip
Hiking time: 3 hours
Elevation gain: 800 feet
Maps: U.S.G.S. Tioga Pass

Summary of hike: The hike to the Gaylor Lakes leads up and across a top-of-the-world alpine plateau. The lakes sit above 10,000 feet in a treeless meadow teaming with wildflowers, babbling creeks, rocky knolls and an endless panorama of mountain peaks in every direction. The hike includes a visit to a stone cabin, built of stacked rock without mortar, and the remains of the Great Sierra Mine, built in the late 1870s. From the mine is a magnificent view south of the two lakes and surrounding peaks.

Driving directions: From the Tuolumne Meadows Visitor Center drive 8.2 miles east on Tioga Road to the Tioga Pass entrance. The parking lot is on the left (west) side of the road 100 feet before reaching the exit station at the park's boundary.

Hiking directions: From the parking lot, the trail heads west, leading uphill through a lodgepole pine forest. The first 0.6 miles is a steep ascent up a rocky trail to a broad open saddle overlooking Middle Gaylor Lake and the majestic peaks that loom in the distance. The trail then descends 200 feet to the lake. Turn right and closely follow the north shore of Middle Gaylor Lake to the inlet stream that links the middle and upper lakes. Cross the stream and continue north (right) along the west edge of the stream until reaching Upper Gaylor Lake. Stay close to the west shore of Upper Gaylor Lake, and continue north, backed by the cone-shaped Gaylor Peak. Head up the hillside en route to the stone cabin and the Great Sierra Mine at the park boundary, which can be seen on Tioga Hill above. The last 0.2 miles to the buildings is a steep climb. To return, follow the same path back.

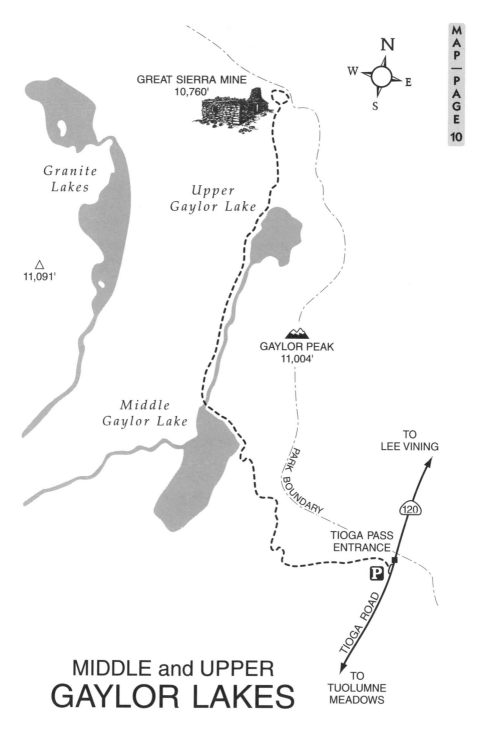

N
W · E
S

GREAT SIERRA MINE
10,760'

Granite Lakes

Upper Gaylor Lake

△ 11,091'

GAYLOR PEAK
11,004'

Middle Gaylor Lake

PARK BOUNDARY

TO LEE VINING

120

TIOGA PASS ENTRANCE

P

TIOGA ROAD

TO TUOLUMNE MEADOWS

MIDDLE and UPPER
GAYLOR LAKES

Hike 2
Lyell Canyon

Hiking distance: 2.2 miles round trip (or up to 15 miles)
Hiking time: 1 hour or more
Elevation gain: Near level
Maps: U.S.G.S. Vogelsang Peak and Tioga Pass

Summary of hike: Lyell Canyon offers a scenic, pastoral hike along a level portion of the Pacific Crest/John Muir Trail. The trail passes through beautiful subalpine meadows along the banks of the Lyell Fork of the Tuolumne River for 8 miles. Early on, the trail crosses the Dana Fork of the Tuolumne River and a double bridge, built into smooth granite slabs over the Lyell Fork by pools and cascades. This easy, meandering path through gorgeous terrain allows you to hike as short or long a distance as you like.

Driving directions: The trailhead is by the Tuolumne Meadows Lodge parking lot. Drive 1.6 miles east of the Tuolumne Meadows Visitor Center on Tioga Road to the lodge turnoff on the right (south). Turn right and continue 0.4 miles to the first parking lot on the left.

If you are camping at Tuolumne Meadows Campground, you may begin the hike at the south end of the A-Campsites. The trail parallels the Lyell Fork for one mile to a junction where the two trails meet near the double bridge over the Lyell Fork.

Hiking directions: From the lodge parking lot, cross the road to the trailhead. Walk east, parallel to the Dana Fork, and cross the bridge. Follow the forested trail 0.5 miles to the double bridge crossing. Just beyond the bridge is a trail junction with the John Muir/Pacific Crest Trail. Take the trail to the left through lodgepole pines, following the Lyell Fork up Lyell Canyon. (The trail to the right leads back one mile to the Tuolumne Meadows Campground.) A half mile up canyon from the junction is a footbridge that crosses Rafferty Creek. This is the turnaround spot for a 2.2-mile hike.

To hike further, the level trail parallels the river through Lyell Canyon for 7 miles before a steep ascent over Donohue Pass. Choose your own turn-around spot.

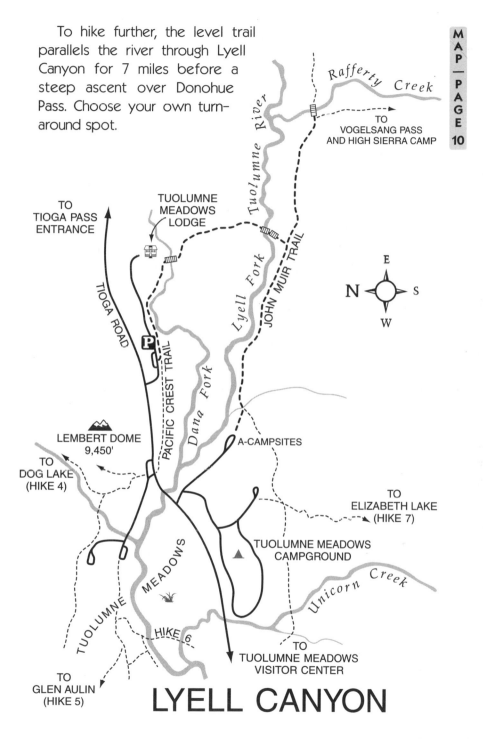

TO
VOGELSANG PASS
AND HIGH SIERRA CAMP

Rafferty Creek

Tuolumne River

TO
TIOGA PASS
ENTRANCE

TUOLUMNE
MEADOWS
LODGE

Lyell Fork

JOHN MUIR TRAIL

E

N   S

W

TIOGA ROAD

P

PACIFIC CREST TRAIL

Dana Fork

LEMBERT DOME
9,450'

TO
DOG LAKE
(HIKE 4)

A-CAMPSITES

TO
ELIZABETH LAKE
(HIKE 7)

TUOLUMNE MEADOWS
CAMPGROUND

TUOLUMNE   MEADOWS

Unicorn Creek

HIKE 6

TO
TUOLUMNE MEADOWS
VISITOR CENTER

TO
GLEN AULIN
(HIKE 5)

LYELL CANYON

Hike 3
Lembert Dome

Hiking distance: 2.8 miles round trip
Hiking time: 2 hours
Elevation gain: 850 feet
Maps: U.S.G.S. Tioga Pass

Summary of hike: Lembert Dome sits at the east end of Tuolumne Meadows. It is an impressive, polished granite dome with a distinctive profile sculpted by glacial ice. From its 9,450-foot elevation, it offers the premiere view of Tuolumne Meadows and the canyon below. From the exposed dome summit, there is a sweeping 360-degree view of the surrounding mountain peaks, including Unicorn Peak, Cathedral Peak, Mount Conness, Mount Dana and Mount Gibbs. The trail up to the north side of the asymmetrical dome is short but steep. Careful footing, especially on the way down, is essential.

Driving directions: From the Tuolumne Meadows Visitor Center, drive 1.2 miles east on Tioga Road to the well-marked trailhead parking lot on the left (north) side of the road.

Hiking directions: From the parking lot, the trail leads north past the restrooms. At 0.1 mile is a posted trail junction. Take the right fork to Lembert Dome. (The left fork leads to Dog Lake, Hike 4.) The trail immediately begins its steep ascent through the lodgepole pine forest around the west flank of Lembert Dome. From the saddle along the north side, the ascent up the bald backside of the dome becomes easier. The dome is not as steep a climb as it appears from below. Choose your own route as you climb south along the dome's bare, terraced surface. There are several levels of the granite dome. From the first ascent onward you are rewarded with spectacular views down canyon. Choose a path to suit your own comfort level. Return along the same trail.

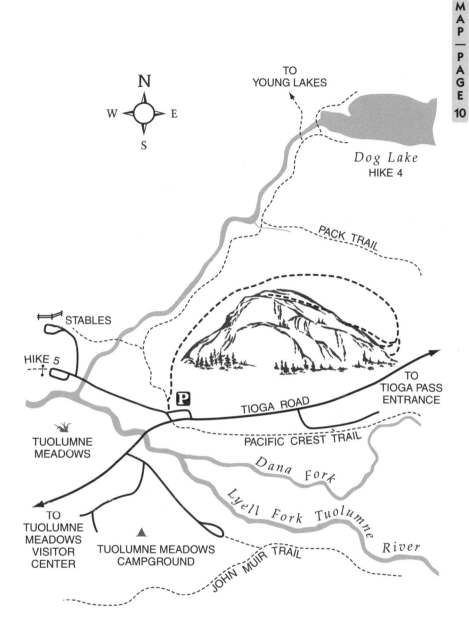

N
W · E
S

TO
YOUNG LAKES

Dog Lake
HIKE 4

PACK TRAIL

STABLES

HIKE 5

TO
TIOGA PASS
ENTRANCE

P

TIOGA ROAD

PACIFIC CREST TRAIL

TUOLUMNE
MEADOWS

Dana Fork

Lyell Fork Tuolumne River

TO
TUOLUMNE
MEADOWS
VISITOR
CENTER

TUOLUMNE MEADOWS
CAMPGROUND

JOHN MUIR TRAIL

LEMBERT DOME

Hike 4
Dog Lake

Hiking distance: 2.4 miles round trip
Hiking time: 1.5 hours
Elevation gain: 600 feet
Maps: U.S.G.S. Tioga Pass

Summary of hike: Dog Lake is a beautiful half-mile-long lake surrounded by grassy meadows and stands of lodgepole pines sitting at 9,240 feet. A smooth, level path circles the lake while mountain peaks rise up in the distance. The grassy terrain, pretty surroundings and eastward views of the Sierra Crest make this a great place for a picnic. The trail to Dog Lake begins at the east end of Tuolumne Meadows near the base of Lembert Dome. The path leads through a lodgepole pine and fir forest to the alpine lake.

Driving directions: From the Tuolumne Meadows Visitor Center, drive 1.2 miles east on Tioga Road to the well-marked trailhead parking lot on the left (north) side of the road.

Hiking directions: From the parking lot, the trail leads north past the restrooms to a trail junction. The Dog Lake Trail goes to the left. (The right fork leads to Lembert Dome, Hike 3.) Head through a small meadow and into the lodgepole forest, passing a trail from the stables on the left at 0.2 miles. From here, the path climbs under the west face of Lembert Dome, gaining over 400 feet in the next half mile. As it levels off, there is a stream crossing to another junction—stay left. (The right fork is a pack trail that leads around the north side of Lembert Dome.) Continue gently uphill to another junction one mile from the trailhead. The left leads to the Young Lakes, 4.9 miles beyond. Bear to the right. From this junction it is 0.2 miles to the west end of Dog Lake. The designated trail leads along the southern shore, although trails lead around the lake in both directions. The east end of the lake is wet and boggy until late in the summer. Return along the same trail.

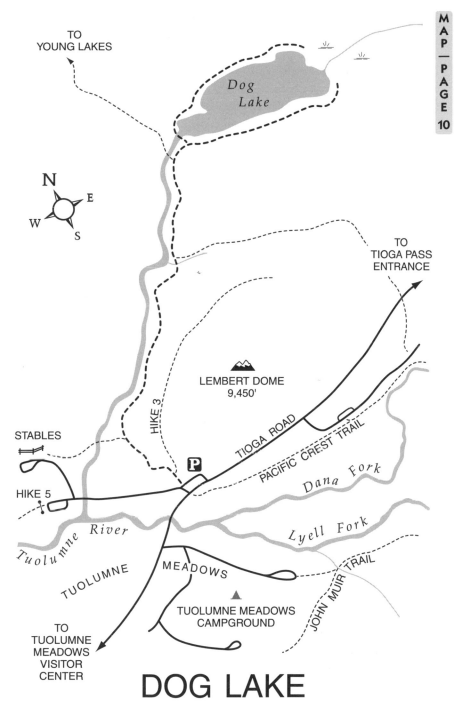

TO
YOUNG LAKES

Dog
Lake

N
E
W
S

TO
TIOGA PASS
ENTRANCE

LEMBERT DOME
9,450'

HIKE 3

STABLES

TIOGA ROAD

PACIFIC CREST TRAIL

Dana Fork

P

HIKE 5

Tuolumne River

Lyell Fork

Tuolu

TUOLUMNE MEADOWS

JOHN MUIR TRAIL

TUOLUMNE MEADOWS
CAMPGROUND

TO
TUOLUMNE
MEADOWS
VISITOR
CENTER

DOG LAKE

Hike 5
Glen Aulin and Tuolumne Falls

Hiking distance: 10.4 miles round trip
Hiking time: 5 hours
Elevation gain: 400 feet
Maps: U.S.G.S. Tioga Pass and Falls Ridge

map
next page

Summary of hike: The Glen Aulin Trail, a portion of the Pacific Crest Trail, is a popular hike that leads to Glen Aulin High Sierra Camp and the Grand Canyon of the Tuolumne River. This hike follows the Tuolumne River through scenic open meadows (cover photo) to Tuolumne Falls and White Cascade. Beyond the meadows, the trail passes magnificent cascades and water- falls all the way to Glen Aulin. Tuolumne Falls and White Cascade are a continuous, powerful 200-foot cascade with foaming pools tumbling down a granite slope. From the top of the falls, the path descends along the raging whitewater of White Cascade and ends at a deep river pool and pebbly beach in Glen Aulin.

Driving directions: From the Tuolumne Meadows Visitor Center, drive 1.2 miles east on Tioga Road to the well-marked Lembert Dome/Dog Lake trailhead parking lot on the left (north) side of the road. Turn left and follow the gravel road 0.3 miles to the parking area by the locked gate.

Hiking directions: Take the unpaved road past the trail gate along the north edge of Tuolumne Meadows. Pass interpretive displays to a signed trail split. The left fork stays in the meadow on Old Tioga Road (Hike 6). Take the right fork above the meadow to an overlook of Soda Springs. Bear to the right at the posted Glen Aulin Trail. Enter the forest and cross Delaney Creek on a log to the right of the trail at 1.4 miles. The near-level path skirts a large meadow on the left to a posted Y-fork at 1.7 miles. The right fork leads to Young Lakes. Take the left fork, reaching the Tuolumne River at the east end of an open, grassy meadow with views of Cathedral and Unicorn peaks. Cross three consecutive branches of Dingley Creek at 2.7 miles and follow the meandering river. The trail alternates from meadows to shady forest to bare granite slabs marked with cairns. Climb around a granite outcrop at the river gorge, and descend to a wooden bridge over the Tuolumne River at 4.1 miles, just upstream from a waterfall. Cross the bridge and follow the west bank of the river to a front view of the raging waterfall. The rock-lined path follows the magnificent cascade to the top of Tuolumne Falls. The path dips through glades and zigzags down to the base of the 100-foot cataract. Follow the roaring river parallel to White Cascade to the May Lake junction on the left at 5.1 miles. Descend to the right and cross a bridge over the river to a 4-way junction. The left fork leads up Glen Aulin valley, passing a series of waterfalls to the Grand Canyon of the Tuolumne River. The right fork crosses a wooden bridge over Conness Creek to a beach near the Glen Aulin High Sierra Camp. From the beach are views of the entire cascade up to Tuolumne Falls.

Hike 6
Tuolumne Meadows and Soda Springs

Hiking distance: 1.5 miles round trip
Hiking time: 1 hour
Elevation gain: Level

map
next page

Maps: U.S.G.S. Vogelsang Peak and Tioga Pass

Summary of hike: Tuolumne Meadows is the largest sub-alpine meadow in the Sierra Nevada. The 2.5-mile-long meadow was formed by a glacier more than 2,000 feet thick. The trail crosses a bridge over the Tuolumne River, which winds through the meadow surrounded by peaks and domes. Soda Springs, located on the north side of the meadow, is a naturally carbonated mineral spring. Pools of mineral water bubble up from beneath the ground. Northwest of Soda Springs is the historic Parsons Memorial Lodge, built entirely from native rock and log in 1915 by the Sierra Club. McCauley Cabin, to its south, is a pioneer structure built in 1817 that is currently used as a ranger residence. This lush meadow is a popular area for swimming and picnicking. You can easily spend the whole day exploring and daydreaming in the meadow.

Driving directions: The trailhead is located 0.1 mile east of the Tuolumne Meadows Visitor Center along the north side of Tioga Road. Parking spaces are available alongside the road.

Hiking directions: From the parking area, the wide trail heads north, directly into the meadow. Continue 0.5 miles to a wooden bridge crossing the Tuolumne River. Across the bridge, continue to the left along the river. A short distance ahead is a junction. Take the trail to the right leading up to Parsons Memorial Lodge and McCauley Cabin. From the lodge, a trail leads east to Soda Springs and an old wooden enclosure on a grassy knoll. From the springs the trail heads back down to the Tuolumne River and the bridge. Additional trails meander along the river and through the meadow.

Soda Springs may also be accessed from the Lembert Dome parking lot.

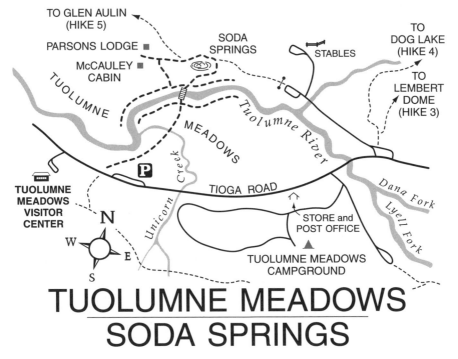

TUOLUMNE MEADOWS
SODA SPRINGS

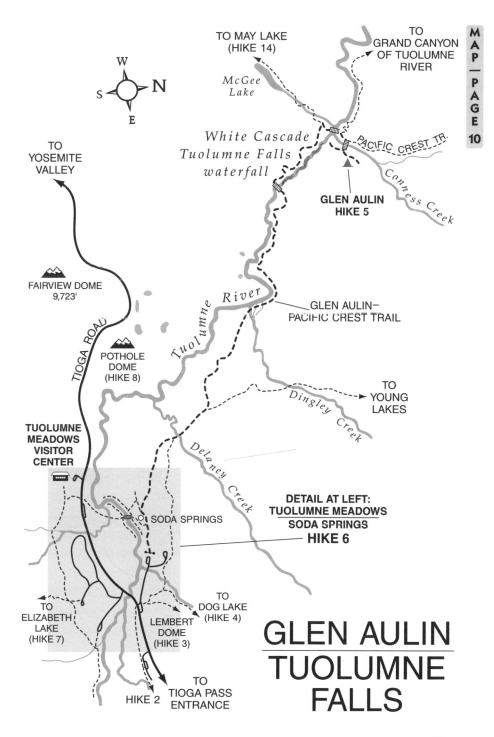

TO MAY LAKE
(HIKE 14)

TO
GRAND CANYON
OF TUOLUMNE
RIVER

*McGee
Lake*

W

N

S

E

White Cascade
Tuolumne Falls
waterfall

PACIFIC CREST TR.

Conness Creek

**GLEN AULIN
HIKE 5**

TO
YOSEMITE
VALLEY

FAIRVIEW DOME
9,723'

Tuolumne River

GLEN AULIN–
PACIFIC CREST TRAIL

TIOGA ROAD

POTHOLE
DOME
(HIKE 8)

TO
YOUNG
LAKES

Dingley Creek

**TUOLUMNE
MEADOWS
VISITOR
CENTER**

Delaney Creek

SODA SPRINGS

**DETAIL AT LEFT:
TUOLUMNE MEADOWS
SODA SPRINGS
HIKE 6**

TO
ELIZABETH
LAKE
(HIKE 7)

TO
DOG LAKE
(HIKE 4)

LEMBERT
DOME
(HIKE 3)

HIKE 2

TO
TIOGA PASS
ENTRANCE

GLEN AULIN
TUOLUMNE
FALLS

Hike 7
Elizabeth Lake

Hiking distance: 4.6 miles round trip
Hiking time: 3 hours
Elevation gain: 800 feet
Maps: U.S.G.S. Vogelsang Peak

Summary of hike: The hike to Elizabeth Lake is a steady climb for the first half of the hike. The trail then parallels Unicorn Creek, which drains Elizabeth Lake, through a beautiful valley. A lush meadow marbled with streams surrounds the lake. The glacially carved granite cliffs of the Cathedral Range form a cirque around the south end of Elizabeth Lake, while the spire of Unicorn Peak towers above to the west. This is a wonderful place to admire the scenery, picnic and explore the delicate shoreline.

Driving directions: The trailhead is located inside the Tuolumne Meadows Campground just off Tioga Road, one mile east of the Tuolumne Meadows Visitor Center. At the campground entrance booth, request a free day-parking permit and campground/trailhead map. The trailhead is located by Campsite B-49.

There is also a trail leading to the trailhead from the Tuolumne Meadows Visitor Center. This route would add one mile to your hike in each direction.

Hiking directions: At the trailhead, head south to a junction with the John Muir Trail, 300 feet ahead. Continue south on the main trail through the shade of a lodgepole pine forest. There is a small stream crossing at 0.5 miles and another crossing at one mile. Just past the second stream, the trail levels off. At 1.2 miles the route meets, then parallels, the cascading waters of Unicorn Creek as you emerge into a lush, green meadow. The trail divides as it approaches the lake. Footpaths lead in both directions along the picturesque shoreline. To return, follow the same path back.

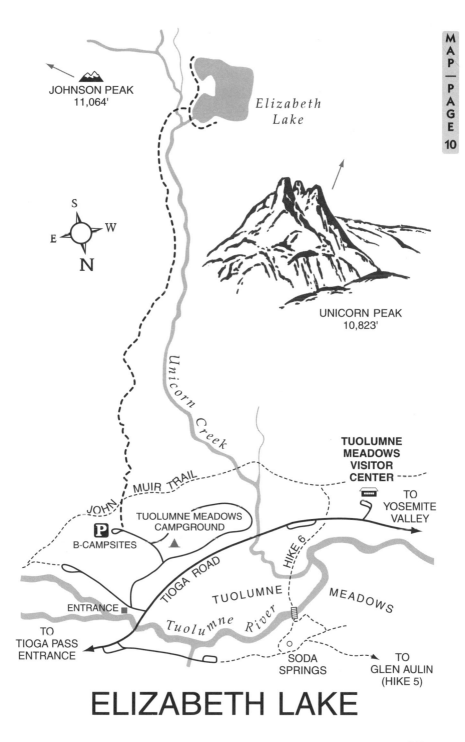

JOHNSON PEAK
11,064'

Elizabeth Lake

S
E — W
N

UNICORN PEAK
10,823'

Unicorn Creek

TUOLUMNE
MEADOWS
VISITOR
CENTER

JOHN MUIR TRAIL

TUOLUMNE MEADOWS
CAMPGROUND

P
B-CAMPSITES

TUOLUMNE

HIKE 6

MEADOWS

TIOGA ROAD

Tuolumne River

TO
YOSEMITE
VALLEY

ENTRANCE

TO
TIOGA PASS
ENTRANCE

SODA
SPRINGS

TO
GLEN AULIN
(HIKE 5)

ELIZABETH LAKE

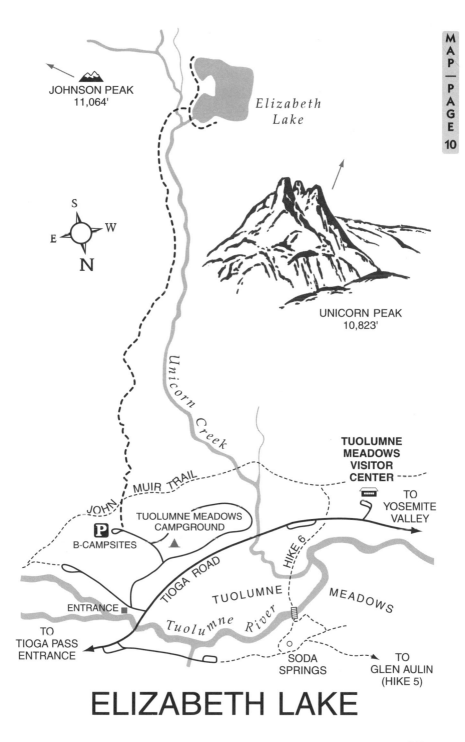
MAP—PAGE 10

Hike 8
Pothole Dome

Hiking distance: 1.1 mile round trip
Hiking time: 45 minutes
Elevation gain: 200 feet
Maps: U.S.G.S. Falls Ridge

Summary of hike: Pothole Dome rests on the west end of Tuolumne Meadows. The trail skirts the edge of the fragile subalpine meadow to the trees at the base of the polished granite dome. The hike ascends the smooth and gentle rock slope past erratics, the rounded boulders that were transported and deposited by retreating glaciers. Flowing waters trapped beneath the glaciers formed the large and numerous potholes. From the 8,760-foot summit are sweeping vistas of Tuolumne Meadows, the Tuolumne River, Lembert Dome, Fairview Dome, Mount Gibbs, Mount Dana and the western part of the Cathedral Range.

Driving directions: From the Tuolumne Meadows Visitor Center, drive 1.2 miles west on Tioga Road to the signed pull-out on the right (north) side of the road.

Hiking directions: From the west end of the parking area, take the well-defined path along the edge of the meadow. At the west end of Pothole Dome, curve right, looping around the perimeter of the meadow to the base of the dome. Follow the foot of the dome on the edge of picturesque Tuolumne Meadows. At the south end of the dome is a trail split. The main trail continues along the west edge of the meadow. Bear left on the side path to ascend Pothole Dome. Choose your own route up the exposed slope, determined by the gradient you prefer. From the summit are 360-degree panoramic views.

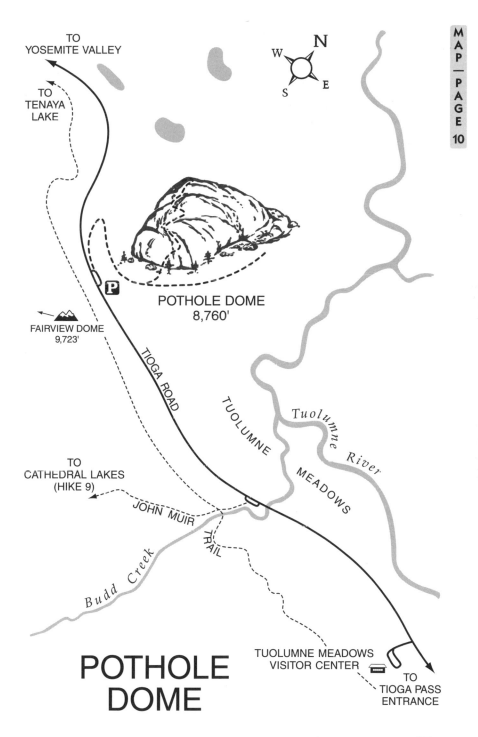

TO
YOSEMITE VALLEY

TO
TENAYA
LAKE

N
W   E
S

POTHOLE DOME
8,760'

P

FAIRVIEW DOME
9,723'

TIOGA ROAD

TUOLUMNE

MEADOWS

Tuolumne River

TO
CATHEDRAL LAKES
(HIKE 9)

JOHN MUIR

TRAIL

Budd Creek

POTHOLE
DOME

TUOLUMNE MEADOWS
VISITOR CENTER

TO
TIOGA PASS
ENTRANCE

Hike 9
Lower Cathedral Lake

Hiking distance: 7 miles round trip
Hiking time: 4 hours
Elevation gain: 1,000 feet
Maps: U.S.G.S. Tenaya Lake

Summary of hike: Lower Cathedral Lake sits at 9,250 feet in a glacial cirque beneath the horned spire of Cathedral Peak. Glaciated mountains curve around the southwest side of the enchanting lake, while bedrock surrounds the lake's perimeter. This subalpine trail up to the lake has views of the Tenaya Lake basin and the smooth, ice-sculpted Fairview Dome. This trail is part of the John Muir Trail.

Driving directions: From the Tuolumne Meadows Visitor Center, drive 0.5 miles west on Tioga Road to the trailhead parking lot on the left (south) side of the road.

Hiking directions: From the parking lot, the trail heads southwest to a junction at 0.1 mile. Continue straight, parallel to Budd Creek. (The intersecting trail connects Tenaya Lake with Tuolumne Meadows.) The trail climbs 550 feet through the dense forest in 0.7 miles, then levels off for a half mile. The trail then skirts the base of Cathedral Peak's northern granite slope. At 1.4 miles cross Cathedral Creek and begin a second ascent, gaining 450 feet in a half mile. As the trail levels, the route passes through an open, sandy forest while the spires of Cathedral Peak come into full view. At three miles is a fork. Take the right branch to Lower Cathedral Lake, 0.5 miles ahead. (The left fork continues along the John Muir Trail to Yosemite Valley, passing Upper Cathedral Lake.) The trail zigzags down the rocky slope, crossing the outlet stream from Upper Cathedral Lake three times to a meadow. Several trails cross to the east shore of the lake by flat rock slabs. Choose your own path as you explore. On the west side are views down the valley to Tenaya Lake and Polly Dome. Return along the same trail.

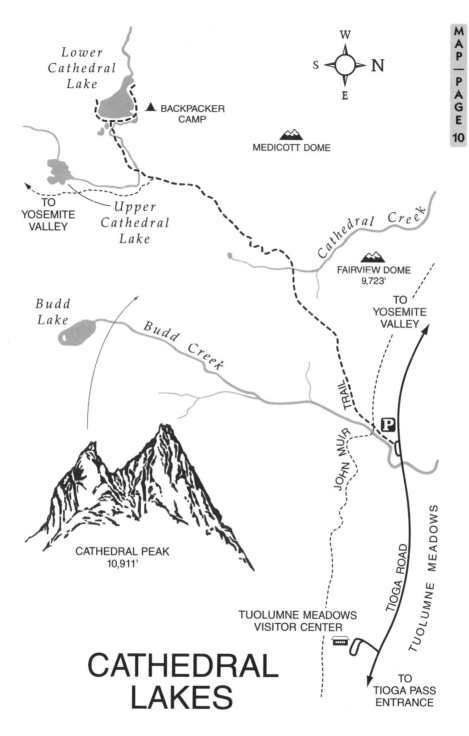

Lower Cathedral Lake

▲ BACKPACKER CAMP

W N S E

MEDICOTT DOME

TO YOSEMITE VALLEY

Upper Cathedral Lake

Cathedral Creek

FAIRVIEW DOME 9,723'

TO YOSEMITE VALLEY

Budd Lake

Budd Creek

JOHN MUIR TRAIL

P

CATHEDRAL PEAK 10,911'

TIOGA ROAD

TUOLUMNE MEADOWS

TUOLUMNE MEADOWS VISITOR CENTER

CATHEDRAL LAKES

TO TIOGA PASS ENTRANCE

Hike 10
Murphy Creek Trail to Polly Dome Lakes

Hiking distance: 5.5 miles round trip
Hiking time: 3 hours
Elevation gain: 500 feet
Maps: U.S.G.S. Tenaya Lake

Summary of hike: The Polly Dome Lakes sit at the base of Polly Dome, an enormous polished granite dome. The hike begins at Tenaya Lake and parallels the east side of Murphy Creek. The trail gently climbs through a shady evergreen forest and crosses a series of bedrock slabs peppered with smooth glacial erratics. The last half mile is off-trail as you pick your way along Murphy Creek to the largest of the Polly Dome Lakes.

Driving directions: From the west end of Tioga Road, drive 31.6 miles east on Tioga Road to the day-use picnic area parking lot on the right at the northeast end of Tenaya Lake. The posted trailhead is directly across the road.

From the Tuolumne Meadows Visitor Center, the parking lot is 7 miles west on the left.

Hiking directions: Cross the highway to the posted Murphy Creek Trail. Enter the Yosemite Wilderness, and climb through the shady lodgepole forest. Parallel Murphy Creek, which cascades down a rock slab shelf. At one mile, cross a tributary stream and traverse large granite slabs dotted with glacial erratics. The trail alternates between the granite slabs, marked with cairns, and forested footpaths. At 1.8 miles, cross Murphy Creek on downfall logs. Follow the west bank of the creek upstream to a pond on the right at 2.3 miles. (If you miss the pond, a posted junction to May Lake is a quarter mile ahead.) The pond is also an excellent destination. To continue to the larger lake, rock hop over the pond's outlet stream. Pick your way east, following the watercourse along the base of Polly Dome. The path emerges at the north end of the shallow, boulder-dotted lake. Return by retracing your steps.

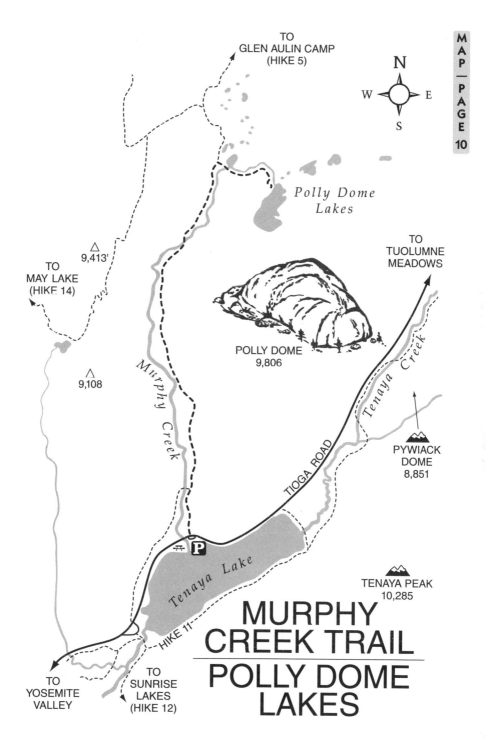

TO
GLEN AULIN CAMP
(HIKE 5)

N
W — E
S

Polly Dome
Lakes

△
9,413'

TO
MAY LAKE
(HIKE 14)

TO
TUOLUMNE
MEADOWS

POLLY DOME
9,806

△
9,108

Murphy Creek

Tenaya Creek

TIOGA ROAD

PYWIACK
DOME
8,851

P

Tenaya Lake

TENAYA PEAK
10,285

MURPHY CREEK TRAIL

HIKE 11

POLLY DOME LAKES

TO
YOSEMITE
VALLEY

TO
SUNRISE
LAKES
(HIKE 12)

Hike 11
Tenaya Lake

Hiking distance: 2.6 miles round trip
Hiking time: 1.5 hours
Elevation gain: Level
Maps: U.S.G.S. Tenaya Lake

Summary of hike: This hike begins at the mile-long Tenaya Lake, one of Yosemite's largest lakes, and follows the southeast shore. Polly Dome sits along the north shore, a steep-sloped granite rock that rises 1,600 feet above the lake. Tenaya Peak towers above to the east. The 150-acre lake has several sandy beaches, including a quarter-mile beach and picnic area along the northeast shore.

Driving directions: From the west end of Tioga Road, drive 31 miles east on Tioga Road to the parking lot on the right at the southwest end of Tenaya Lake. This is the site of the former Tenaya Lake Campground.

From the Tuolumne Meadows Visitor Center, the parking lot is 7.7 miles west on the left.

Hiking directions: The trail begins at the southwest end of Tenaya Lake. Head east along the campground road towards Tenaya Creek, the Tenaya Lake outlet. After crossing, take the trail to the left, staying close to the south shore of Tenaya Lake. (The trail to the right heads to the Sunrise Lakes, Hike 12.) The near-level trail closely follows the perimeter of the lake through a forest of fir, spruce and pine. At the north end of the lake is Tenaya Creek again, the lake's inlet. Cross the creek to the sandy beach along the northeast side of the lake. From the beach, return by taking the same trail back. The views of the surrounding mountains are equally rewarding on the return trip.

You may also complete the loop around the lake on Tioga Road.

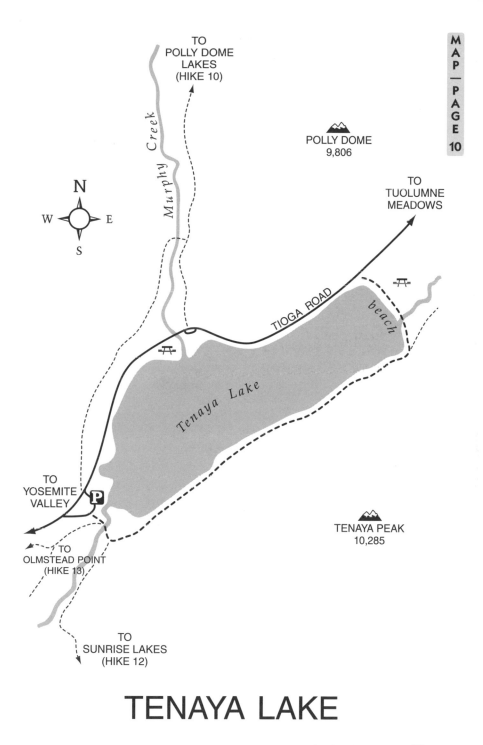

TO
POLLY DOME
LAKES
(HIKE 10)

Murphy Creek

POLLY DOME
9,806

TO
TUOLUMNE
MEADOWS

N
W E
S

TIOGA ROAD

beach

Tenaya Lake

TO
YOSEMITE
VALLEY

P

TENAYA PEAK
10,285

TO
OLMSTEAD POINT
(HIKE 13)

TO
SUNRISE LAKES
(HIKE 12)

TENAYA LAKE

Hike 12
Sunrise Lakes

Hiking distance: 8 miles round trip
Hiking time: 4—5 hours
Elevation gain: 1,000 feet
Maps: U.S.G.S. Tenaya Lake

Summary of hike: The Sunrise Lakes are a series of three beautiful mountain lakes. The trail has a steep one-mile ascent on the east slope of Tenaya Canyon, in which most of the elevation gain is achieved. There are dramatic panoramic views along the way. From the ridgetop are vistas of Mount Hoffman, Tuolumne Peak and a unique view of Half Dome, Clouds Rest and Yosemite Valley.

Driving directions: Same as Tenaya Lake, Hike 11.

Hiking directions: The trail begins at the southwest end of Tenaya Lake. Head east along the road towards Tenaya Creek. After crossing, take the trail to the right, descending into Tenaya Canyon through a pine and fir forest parallel to Tenaya Creek. At all the posted trail junctions, head towards Sunrise H.S.C., the high sierra camp located beyond the lakes. At 1.5 miles the trail begins a steep climb out of the canyon, gaining more than 800 feet in one mile via a series of switchbacks. At the crest is a trail junction. Straight ahead leads to Clouds Rest. Take a short detour to the right of the junction along an unmarked trail. About 300 yards southwest is a commanding view of Yosemite Valley and Half Dome.

Back at the main junction, take the left (northeast) fork. It is an easy half mile to the first of the Sunrise Lakes, backed by a granite cliff. The trail winds along the west shore of Lower Sunrise Lake, crossing the lake's outlet stream. In the next mile, the trail continues gently uphill to the middle and upper lakes. The middle lake is off to the left—a short spur trail will lead you there. The main trail skirts along the southwest shore of Upper Sunrise Lake, the largest of the lakes and our turnaround point.

To hike further, the trail continues to the Sunrise High Sierra Camp and a junction with the John Muir Trail 1.5 miles further. To return, retrace your steps.

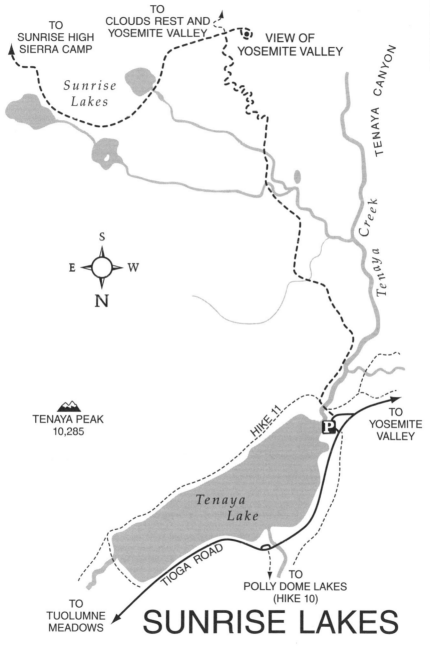

TO
SUNRISE HIGH
SIERRA CAMP

TO
CLOUDS REST AND
YOSEMITE VALLEY

VIEW OF
YOSEMITE VALLEY

Sunrise
Lakes

TENAYA CANYON

Tenaya Creek

S
E —⊙— W
N

TENAYA PEAK
10,285

HIKE 11

P

TO
YOSEMITE
VALLEY

Tenaya
Lake

TIOGA ROAD

TO
POLLY DOME LAKES
(HIKE 10)

TO
TUOLUMNE
MEADOWS

SUNRISE LAKES

Hike 13
Olmsted Point

Hiking distance: 0.5 miles round trip
Hiking time: 20 minutes
Elevation gain: 80 feet
Maps: U.S.G.S. Tenaya Lake

Summary of hike: Olmsted Point is on a polished granite dome with scattered Jeffrey pines, lodgepole pines and glacial erratics. The randomly strewn boulders were left behind after the glaciers retreated more than 10,000 years ago. This short hike begins from a scenic overlook with interpretive panels describing the geologic and scenic features. The trail leads to an 8,400-foot glaciated knoll with breathtaking views. The scenic vistas extend down Tenaya Canyon to the 9,926-foot Clouds Rest, a rounded back view of Half Dome, Mount Watkins, Polly Dome, Tenaya Lake, the domes and peaks of the Tuolumne Meadows region, and the Sierra Crest on the eastern boundary of Yosemite.

Driving directions: From the west end of Tioga Road, drive 29.5 miles east on Tioga Road to the signed parking pullout on the right.
From the Tuolumne Meadows Visitor Center the parking lot is 9.1 miles west on the left.

Hiking directions: From the interpretive panel and overlook, take the rock-lined path downhill. Pass large boulders to a signed 4-way junction. The left fork skirts Tioga Road to Tenaya Lake; the right fork leads to Yosemite Valley via Tenaya Canyon. Walk straight ahead on the nature trail, and curve to the right. Wind through groves of pines, white fir, oak scrub, manzanita and juniper. Ascend the rise and cross a field of erratics to the summit of Olmsted Point on the west rim of Tenaya Canyon. Views down the enormous granite-walled canyon lead to Yosemite Valley. After savoring the surrealistic views of the glacier-scoured landscape, return along the same path.

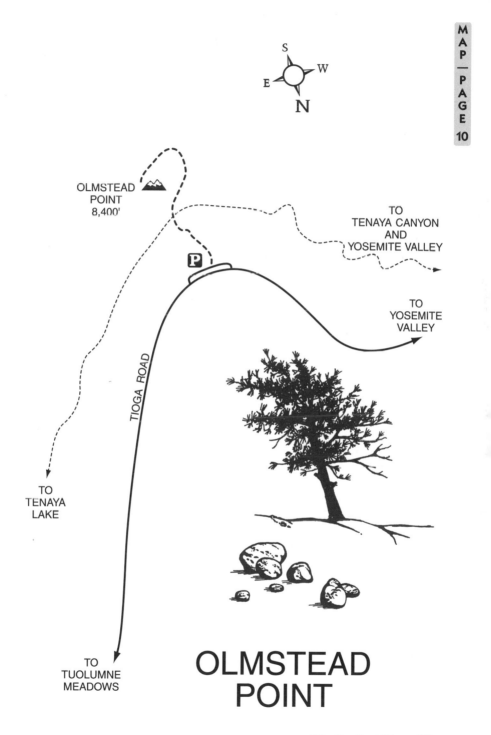

S W
E N

OLMSTEAD
POINT
8,400'

TO
TENAYA CANYON
AND
YOSEMITE VALLEY

TO
YOSEMITE
VALLEY

TIOGA ROAD

TO
TENAYA
LAKE

TO
TUOLUMNE
MEADOWS

OLMSTEAD POINT

Hike 14
May Lake

Hiking distance: 2.4 miles round trip
Hiking time: 1.5 hours
Elevation gain: 450 feet
Maps: U.S.G.S. Tenaya Lake

Summary of hike: May Lake is nestled beneath the towering eastern wall of Mount Hoffman. Located in the center of Yosemite, Mount Hoffman rises more than 1,500 feet out of May Lake to a height of 10,850 feet. The trail offers views of Tenaya Canyon, Cathedral Peak, Half Dome and Clouds Rest. The forested lake is home to the May Lake High Sierra Camp and is a popular trout fishing lake.

Driving directions: From the west end of Tioga Road, drive 27 miles east on Tioga Road to the May Lake turnoff on the left. Turn left and drive 1.8 miles to the trailhead parking lot at the end of the road.

From the Tuolumne Meadows Visitor Center, drive 11.4 miles west to the May Lake turnoff on the right. Turn right and drive 1.8 miles to the trailhead parking lot.

Hiking directions: The trailhead is to the left (southwest) of a glacial tarn. Cross the bridge and begin hiking north. The trail steadily gains elevation but is not steep. The trail passes through an open forest dominated by lodgepole pine and red fir, allowing plenty of sunlight to filter in through the trees. Portions of the trail cross large slabs of granite dotted with lodgepole pines. The path climbs over granite slabs and reaches a saddle overlooking May Lake. Descend to the lake's southern shore. Just before reaching May Lake is a trail fork. The left fork follows the south end of the lake by the backpacker camp. The right fork follows the east side of the lake, passing May Lake High Sierra Camp. Return along the same trail.

To hike further, the trail continues into the backcountry to Ten Lakes and Glen Aulin.

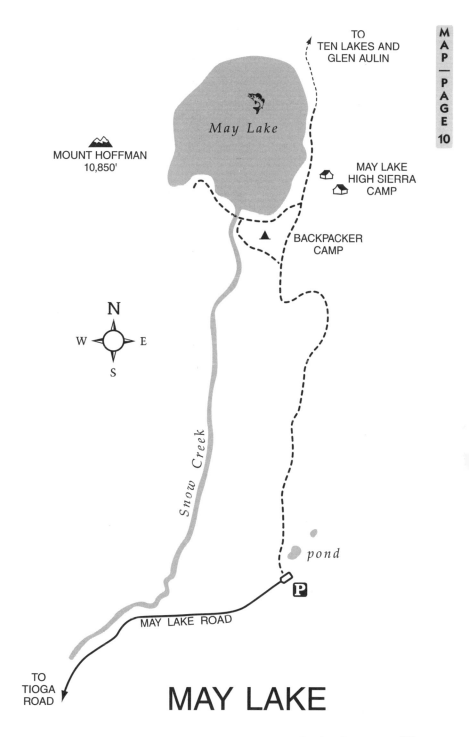

TO
TEN LAKES AND
GLEN AULIN

May Lake

MOUNT HOFFMAN
10,850'

MAY LAKE
HIGH SIERRA
CAMP

BACKPACKER
CAMP

N
W ⊕ E
S

Snow Creek

pond

P

MAY LAKE ROAD

TO
TIOGA
ROAD

MAY LAKE

Hike 15
Porcupine Creek Trail
to Indian Ridge Natural Arch

Hiking distance: 6.4 miles round trip
Hiking time: 3 hours
Elevation gain: 600 feet
Maps: U.S.G.S. Yosemite Falls

map
next page

Summary of hike: Indian Ridge Natural Arch is a massive, sculpted rock formation with a thin, delicate 20-foot rock arch at its crest. Views from Yosemite's only natural stone arch extend across Indian Ridge to North Dome, Half Dome, Clouds Rest and the Clark Range. The hike follows the Porcupine Creek Trail through a pine and fir forest.

Driving directions: From the west end of Tioga Road, drive 25 miles east on Tioga Road to the signed parking pullout on the right.

From the Tuolumne Meadows Visitor Center, the parking area is 13.6 miles west on the left.

Hiking directions: From the west end of the parking area, take the blocked-off, eroded asphalt road downhill a quarter mile to the end of the pavement. Continue winding through the forest to the former site of the Porcupine Creek Campground. At 0.7 miles, rock hop over a tributary stream of Porcupine Creek, and cross a log over Porcupine Creek to the right of the path. Follow the near-level grade through a small grassy meadow and red fir forest. Rock-hop over another tributary stream to a posted 3-way junction at 1.5 miles. The Snow Creek Trail veers left to Yosemite Valley via Tenaya Canyon (Hike 35). Stay to the right to a second junction 20 yards ahead. The right fork leads to Yosemite Falls (Hike 32). Take the left fork towards North Dome and traverse the hillside. Cross a stream, curve left and climb the hillside to a saddle on Indian Ridge and a posted junction at just under 3 miles. The right fork leads to North Dome (Hike 16). Bear left and zigzag a quarter mile up the steep hillside path to the natural arch. Curve around the east side of the formation with views upward of the arch. From the north side of the rock, climb into the window beneath the arch. After savoring the views, return to the Porcupine Creek Trail and retrace your steps. To hike to North Dome, continue with the next hike.

Hike 16
North Dome

Hiking distance: 8.8 miles round trip
Hiking time: 4.5 hours
Elevation gain: 650 feet
Maps: U.S.G.S. Yosemite Falls

map
next page

Summary of hike: North Dome, a 7,542-foot granite promontory on the north rim, offers the best close-up view there is of Half Dome and Clouds Rest. The bald, polished dome sits 3,571 feet above the Yosemite Valley, with captivating panoramas of the valley, Tenaya Canyon, Glacier Point, Sentinel Dome, Liberty Cap, Panorama Cliff and Illilouette Fall. Two routes from Yosemite Valley also access North Dome, but both routes are very strenuous—Yosemite Falls Trail (Hike 32) and Tenaya Canyon (Hike 35). This hike follows the third and easiest route to North Dome via the Porcupine Creek Trail beginning from Tioga Road.

Driving directions: Same as Hike 15.

Hiking directions: Follow the hiking directions for Hike 15 to the saddle and the signed junction to the Indian Ridge Natural Arch. Take the trail south towards North Dome. Descend along the crest of Indian Ridge to magnificent views of the surrounding peaks. As you near the ridge's point, the path curves left, descending to North Dome. Before curving downhill, detour straight ahead onto the ridge's nose to a spectacular overlook of North Dome, Yosemite Valley and close views of Clouds Rest and Half Dome. Return to the trail and leave Indian Ridge, curving east into the forest and returning to the ridgeline below. Follow the ridge south on huge granite slabs, passing to the right of Basket Dome to a signed junction. The right fork leads to Yosemite Falls (Hike 32). Stay to the left and descend rock steps to the base of North Dome. Ascend the bare rock dome to the rounded summit of North Dome. Just beyond the summit are the best views of Yosemite's granite monoliths, rounded domes, towering pinnacles and merging canyons. Return along the same trail.

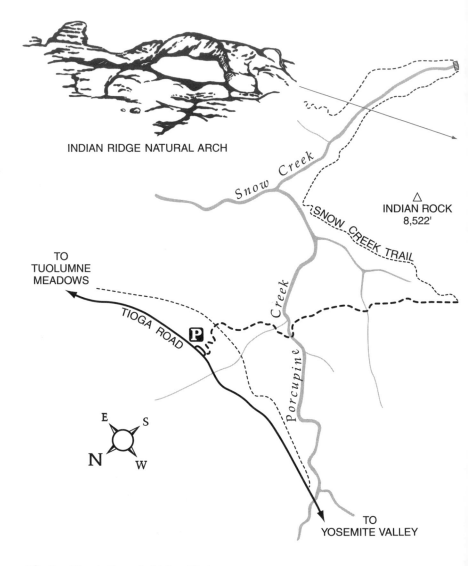

INDIAN RIDGE NATURAL ARCH

Snow Creek

△ INDIAN ROCK 8,522'

SNOW CREEK TRAIL

TO TUOLUMNE MEADOWS

TIOGA ROAD

P

Creek

Porcupine

E S N W

TO YOSEMITE VALLEY

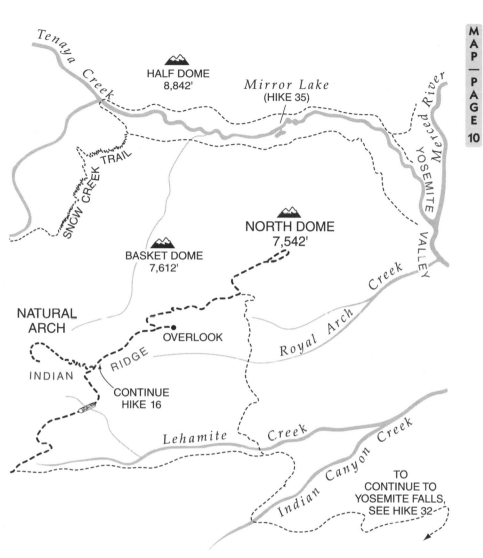

HALF DOME
8,842'

Mirror Lake
(HIKE 35)

Tenaya Creek

Merced River

SNOW CREEK TRAIL

NORTH DOME
7,542'

BASKET DOME
7,612'

NATURAL
ARCH

OVERLOOK

Royal Arch Creek

RIDGE

INDIAN

CONTINUE
HIKE 16

Lehamite Creek

Indian Canyon Creek

YOSEMITE VALLEY

TO
CONTINUE TO
YOSEMITE FALLS,
SEE HIKE 32

POCUPINE CREEK TRAIL TO
INDIAN RIDGE
NATURAL ARCH
NORTH DOME
HIKES 15–16

Hike 17
Yosemite Creek Trail from
Tioga Road to Yosemite Creek Campground

Hiking distance: 4.8 miles round trip
Hiking time: 2.5 hours
Elevation gain: 400 feet
Maps: U.S.G.S. Yosemite Falls

Summary of hike: The Yosemite Creek Trail follows along Yosemite Creek 8 miles from Tioga Road to the viewpoint at the brink of Yosemite Falls. This hike follows the first 2.4 miles of the trail, which descends through a gorgeous, open lodgepole pine forest to a bridge crossing Yosemite Creek. The wide path parallels the creek, following an easy grade to the north end of Yosemite Creek Campground.

Driving directions: From the west end of Tioga Road, drive 19.6 miles east on Tioga Road to the large parking turnout on the right.

From the Tuolumne Meadows Visitor Center the parking turnout is 19 miles west on the left.

Hiking directions: Walk 80 yards west on Tioga Road to the signed trail on the left. Cross a tributary steam and head into the lush forest. Gradually descend while meandering past glacier-carved slabs of granite. Pass a pond on the right, and zigzag down to Yosemite Creek at 0.8 miles. Cross the creek on a downfall log or wade across. Continue south across a trickling stream, and arrive back at the banks of Yosemite Creek alongside a steep granite wall. Parallel the clear creek downstream. Ascend a hill, moving away from the creek, and drop into the upper end of Yosemite Creek Campground at 1.8 miles. Follow the campground road along the creek 0.6 miles to two consecutive bridge crossings and a signed trail on the left. This is our turnaround spot.

To hike further, the trail follows Yosemite Creek south, reaching the top of Yosemite Falls 5.6 miles ahead.

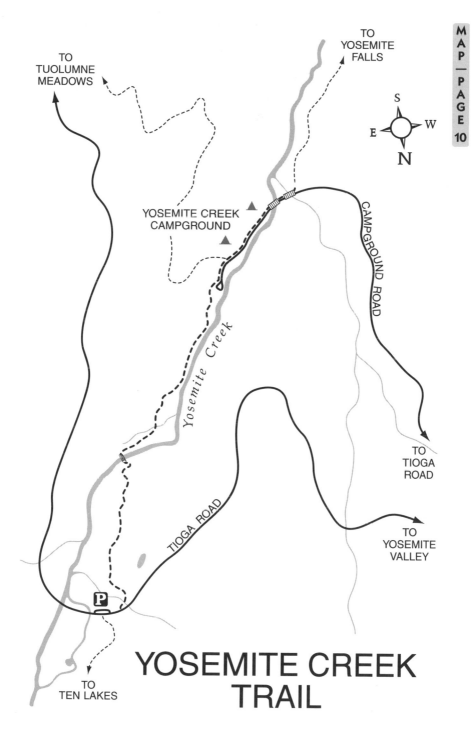

TO TUOLUMNE MEADOWS

TO YOSEMITE FALLS

S
E — W
N

YOSEMITE CREEK CAMPGROUND

Yosemite Creek

CAMPGROUND ROAD

TO TIOGA ROAD

TO YOSEMITE VALLEY

TIOGA ROAD

P

TO TEN LAKES

YOSEMITE CREEK TRAIL

Hike 18
Harden Lake

Hiking distance: 6 miles round trip
Hiking time: 3 hours
Elevation gain: 450 feet
Maps: U.S.G.S. Tamarack Flat and Hetch Hetchy Reservoir

Summary of hike: The trail to Harden Lake follows the original Tioga Road built in 1883. It was closed to vehicles in 1961 when the current Tioga Road was completed. The hike parallels the Middle Fork of the Tuolumne River downstream through a beautiful pine forest past small cascades and pools. Nine-acre Harden Lake, at an elevation of 7,600 feet, is a popular but uncrowded fishing and picnicking spot.

Driving directions: From the west end of Tioga Road, drive 14.5 miles east on Tioga Road to the White Wolf Campground turnoff on the left. Turn left and drive one mile to the White Wolf Lodge. Park near the lodge.

From the Tuolumne Meadows Visitor Center, drive 24 miles west to the White Wolf Campground turnoff and turn right.

Hiking directions: From White Wolf Lodge, walk down the road to the north, passing the campground. The road (no longer accessible to vehicles) crosses a bridge over the Middle Fork of the Tuolumne River. For the next mile the trail gradually descends, parallel to the east bank of the river. At 1.6 miles a posted footpath to Harden Lake branches off to the right. The footpath crosses the slope of a glacial moraine through a forest of pine, fir and aspen. You may stay on the road or take the footpath. They connect again 0.7 miles ahead. If you choose the road, there is another fork in the road to the left 0.3 miles past the footpath junction. After the two routes merge, follow the road another quarter mile to a posted junction to Harden Lake. (The left trail continues along the original Tioga Road to Smith Meadow and Hetch Hetchy Road.) Take the right fork to the south end of Harden Lake and a trail split. Explore the perimeter of the lake on trails of use. The main trail curves to the east side of the lake and steeply descends for miles into the Grand Canyon of the Tuolumne River. Return along the same trail.

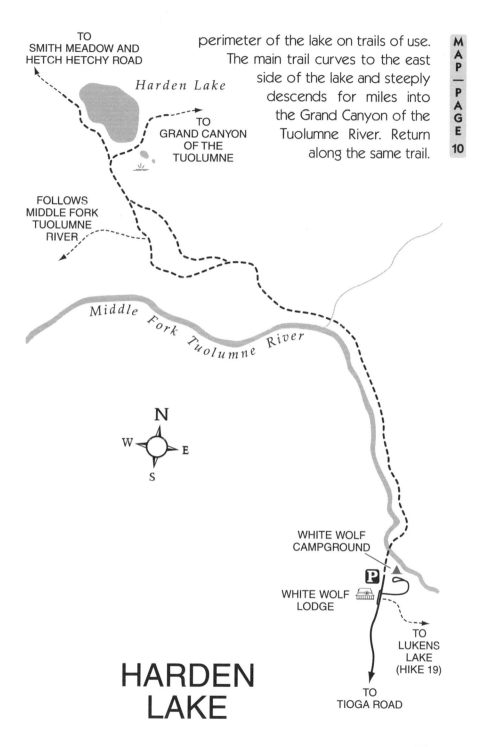

TO
SMITH MEADOW AND
HETCH HETCHY ROAD

Harden Lake

TO
GRAND CANYON
OF THE
TUOLUMNE

FOLLOWS
MIDDLE FORK
TUOLUMNE
RIVER

Middle Fork Tuolumne River

N
W   E
S

WHITE WOLF
CAMPGROUND

WHITE WOLF
LODGE

TO
LUKENS
LAKE
(HIKE 19)

HARDEN
LAKE

TO
TIOGA ROAD

Hike 19
Lukens Lake

Hiking distance: 4.6 miles round trip or 1.6 miles round trip
Hiking time: 2.5 hours or 1 hour
Elevation gain: 250 feet or 150 feet
Maps: U.S.G.S. Tamarack Flat and Yosemite Falls

Summary of hike: Lukens Lake is a scenic mountain lake with forests along one side and beautiful meadows covered in wild-flowers along the other. Two routes access the lake. Both trails are easy hikes that lead through lush forests. The longer route begins at White Wolf Lodge. The shorter route begins along Tioga Road.

Driving directions: To start from White Wolf Lodge, follow the same driving directions as Hike 18, parking near the lodge.

The trailhead for the shorter hike is on Tioga Road 1.8 miles east of the White Wolf turnoff. Park on the south side of the road. From the Tuolumne Meadows Visitor Center, the trailhead is 22 miles west on Tioga Road.

Hiking directions: The posted trailhead at White Wolf is directly across the road from the lodge. Head east through a lodgepole pine forest along the south edge of the camp-ground. At 0.7 miles is a log crossing over the Middle Fork of the Tuolumne River. At 0.9 miles is a posted trail junction. The left fork leads to Harden Lake. Take the right fork, which paral-lels the river for the next mile to another junction. The left fork parallels the Middle Fork and leads to Ten Lakes. Again take the right fork, and ford the Middle Fork. Continue uphill to the north shore of Lukens Lake. The trail parallels the lake along the east shore, then leads down to the trailhead on Tioga Road. To return, retrace your steps.

From the pullout on Tioga Road, the trail heads north from the highway through a white pine and red fir forest to a saddle. Descend to a wet meadow at the south end of Lukens Lake, joining the longer trail from the west.

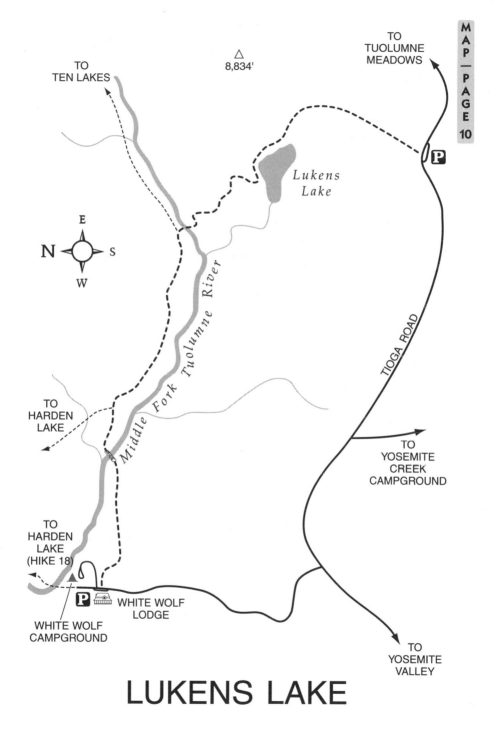

TO
TUOLUMNE
MEADOWS

TO
TEN LAKES

△
8,834'

*Lukens
Lake*

P

N

E

S

W

Middle Fork Tuolumne River

TIOGA ROAD

TO
HARDEN
LAKE

TO
YOSEMITE
CREEK
CAMPGROUND

TO
HARDEN
LAKE
(HIKE 18)

P

WHITE WOLF
LODGE

WHITE WOLF
CAMPGROUND

TO
YOSEMITE
VALLEY

LUKENS LAKE

Hike 20
Cascade Creek from Tamarack Campground

Hiking distance: 5 miles round trip
Hiking time: 2.5 hours
Elevation gain: 350 feet
Maps: U.S.G.S. Tamarack Flat and El Capitan

Summary of hike: The trail to Cascade Creek is a quiet, secluded hike along the original Big Oak Flat Road that led to Yosemite Valley back in 1874. The abandoned road has been closed to vehicles since landslides blocked its path in 1945. The trail passes through a cedar, fir and pine forest and a stunning boulder field to a bridge crossing Cascade Creek.

Driving directions: From the west end of Tioga Road, drive 3.7 miles east on Tioga Road to the Tamarack Campground turnoff on the right. Turn right and drive 3 miles to the end of the unmaintained road. Park where available.

From the Tuolumne Meadows Visitor Center, drive 34.8 miles west to the Tamarack Campground turnoff on the left.

Hiking directions: The trailhead is at the south end of the campground. Walk past the gate to the old abandoned asphalt road that leads through the forest. At 0.5 miles, the trail crosses a tributary of Tamarack Creek. At one mile the trail begins its descent. The display of boulders in this area is magnificent. The trail crosses a tributary of Cascade Creek, then follows it downstream to the bridge crossing Cascade Creek. There are numerous cascades along the creek before reaching the bridge. This is our turnaround spot. One mile below the bridge, Tamarack and Cascade Creeks merge. Just below their confluence, the creek tumbles 500 feet in a long cascade called The Cascades (Hike 30).

To hike further, the trail continues east to the summit of El Capitan at 8 miles and on to Yosemite Point and North Dome.

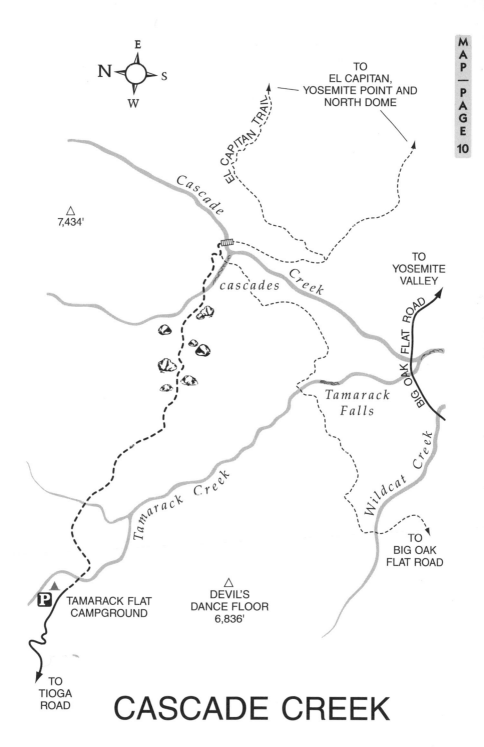

E
N — S
W

TO
EL CAPITAN,
YOSEMITE POINT AND
NORTH DOME

EL CAPITAN TRAIL

Cascade

△
7,434'

Creek

cascades

TO
YOSEMITE
VALLEY

BIG OAK FLAT ROAD

Tamarack
Falls

Wildcat Creek

Tamarack Creek

TO
BIG OAK
FLAT ROAD

P ▲ TAMARACK FLAT
CAMPGROUND

△
DEVIL'S
DANCE FLOOR
6,836'

TO
TIOGA
ROAD

CASCADE CREEK

Hike 21
Tuolumne Grove of Giant Sequoias
Old Big Oak Flat Road

Hiking distance: 2.5 miles round trip
Hiking time: 1.5 hours
Elevation gain: 500 feet
Maps: U.S.G.S. Ackerson Mountain

Summary of hike: This hike follows a portion of the Old Big Oak Flat Road, closed to vehicles in 1993. The historic 6-mile road once connected the Big Oak Flat Entrance with Yosemite Valley. Now a hiking trail, the winding road descends through an intimate old forest of incense cedar, sugar pine, white fir and Douglas fir, reaching the Tuolumne Grove of giant sequoias at one mile. A nature trail begins at the picnic area, once used as a parking lot for viewing the trees. The half-mile trail with interpretive panels loops through the grove of twenty-five giant sequoias. Included is a walk through the Tunnel Tree (also called Dead Giant), a dead but standing tree trunk that was tunneled for horse-drawn wagons in 1878.

Driving directions: From the west end of Tioga Road, drive 0.5 miles eastbound on Tioga Road to the signed parking lot on the left.

Hiking directions: Walk to the far north end of the parking lot, and pass the trailhead gate. Take the old road into the dense forest. The serpentine road steadily winds downhill through the old-growth forest. At one mile the trail enters the Tuolumne Grove. A short distance ahead is a trail split. On the left is a massive sequoia with a viewing deck. Take the upper trail to the right, passing groves of giant sequoias on both sides of the path. Walk through the dead but standing Tunnel Tree. The two trails rejoin at a nature trail loop by the old parking lot. Bear right on the nature trail, and cross a wooden footbridge over the stream. The path follows the 200-foot length of the downed Leaning Tower Tree. Interpretive displays describe the effects

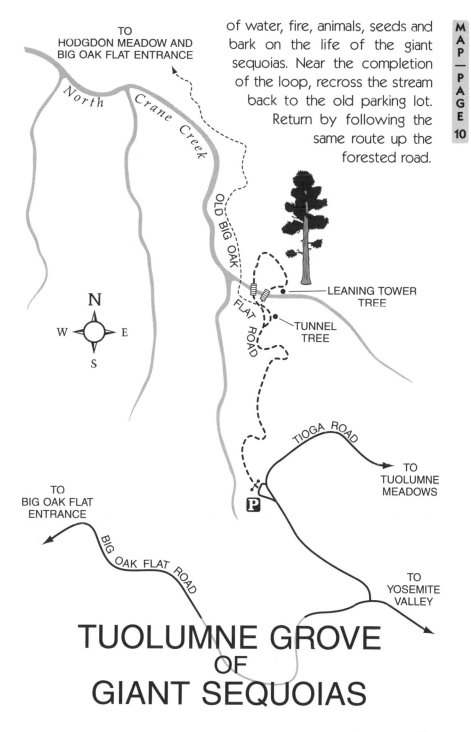

of water, fire, animals, seeds and bark on the life of the giant sequoias. Near the completion of the loop, recross the stream back to the old parking lot. Return by following the same route up the forested road.

TO
HODGDON MEADOW AND
BIG OAK FLAT ENTRANCE

North *Crane Creek*

OLD BIG OAK FLAT ROAD

N
W — E
S

LEANING TOWER TREE

TUNNEL TREE

TIOGA ROAD

TO
TUOLUMNE
MEADOWS

TO
BIG OAK FLAT
ENTRANCE

P

BIG OAK FLAT ROAD

TO
YOSEMITE
VALLEY

TUOLUMNE GROVE
OF
GIANT SEQUOIAS

Hike 22
Wapama Falls

Hiking distance: 4.8 miles round trip
Hiking time: 2.5 hours
Elevation gain: 300 feet
Maps: U.S.G.S. Lake Eleanor

map
next page

Summary of hike: The Hetch Hetchy Valley sits near the western corner of Yosemite, submerged under the Hetch Hetchy Reservoir. Backed up by O'Shaughnessy Dam, the Tuolumne River now floods the Valley. The dam was built in 1914 to provide a water supply to San Francisco. It raised the water level 312 feet above the riverbed, which extends up the valley more than eight miles. The hike to Wapama Falls begins from O'Shaughnessy Dam at the west end of the reservoir. A well-maintained trail follows the reservoir's north shore. The trail passes the 1,000-foot wispy ribbon of seasonal Tueeulala Falls en route to the base of the wide and thick Wapama Falls on Falls Creek. The raging whitewater of Wapama Falls plummets 1,400 feet over a granite precipice and tumbles into the reservoir. Watch for rattlesnakes

Driving directions: From the Big Oak Flat entrance station on Highway 120, drive one mile west (outside the park) to Evergreen Road, the first turnoff on the right. Turn right and continue 7.4 miles to a T-junction at the end of the road. Turn right on Hetch Hetchy Road, and drive 1.3 miles to the Hetch Hetchy entrance station. Enter the park and continue 8 miles to a one-way loop at the end of the road. The parking area is at the far end of the loop, just past O'Shaughnessy Dam.

Hiking directions: Walk downhill to the dam, crossing an overlook of the Hetch Hetchy Reservoir. Wapama Falls, the destination of this hike, can be seen from the trailhead to the left of Hetch Hetchy Dome. Cross the top of O'Shaughnessy Dam. Walk through a 500-foot tunnel, carved through the granite mountain, to the posted Hetch Hetchy trailhead. The wide path winds along the western edge of the reservoir, following the contours of the mountains. The path gains elevation to magnificent vistas of the reservoir and sculpted mountains. At 0.9 miles is a posted junction. The left fork climbs the mountain to Laurel Lake, 7.6 miles ahead. Take the right fork on the Rancheria Falls Trail, staying close to the reservoir on the wide rock shelf. Cross a bridge below seasonal Tueeulala Falls at 1.5 miles, and continue along the talus slopes below the vertical cliffs. Cobblestone steps zigzag down to the base of two-tiered Wapama Falls, where a series of five wood and steel bridges span the boulders over the churning whitewater of Falls Creek. The bridges offer varying views of the foaming rapids beneath your feet. This is our turnaround spot.

To hike further, the trail contours the cliffs parallel to the reservoir to Rancheria Falls 4.2 miles ahead.

Hike 23
O'Shaughnessy Dam to Tuolumne River

Hiking distance: 2 miles round trip
Hiking time: 1 hour
Elevation gain: 250 feet
Maps: U.S.G.S. Lake Eleanor

map
next page

Summary of hike: The O'Shaughnessy Dam rises 312 feet above the Tuolumne River and extends 910 feet between canyon walls at the west end of Hetch Hetchy Valley. The valley is now submerged beneath the Hetch Hetchy Reservoir, which covers 1,861 acres of the narrow, rugged canyon with high granite walls. This hike follows a vehicle-restricted road from the top of O'Shaughnessy Dam to the Tuolumne River at the base of the dam, where a roaring spillway feeds the lower river canyon. The trail continues through the deep granite gorge parallel to the river. Watch for rattlesnakes.

Driving directions: Same as Wapama Falls, Hike 22.

Hiking directions: Walk downhill to O'Shaughnessy Dam,

looking across the clear blue water of Hetch Hetchy Reservoir. Bear left on the paved maintenance road, and pass through the metal gate. Follow the descending road between the rock wall on the left and the narrow canyon and spillway on the right. The pavement soon ends as the road weaves downhill above the Tuolumne River. Just before reaching the tree groves on the canyon floor, the road forks. Take the right fork, heading upstream past lichen-covered boulders to the end of the road in a deep rock gorge at the base of the dam. A column of

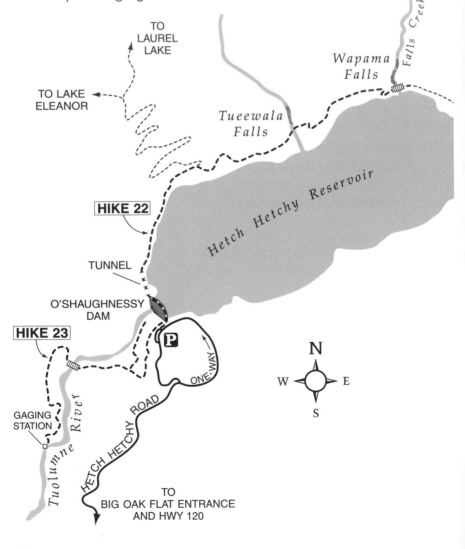

whitewater shoots out of the dam, smashing into the canyon wall. The area may be covered with mist depending on the amount of water being released from the dam. Return to the road fork, and bear right along the valley floor. Cross a bridge over the Tuolumne River in a rock gorge. This is a good turn-around spot.

To hike further, continue another mile to the end of the trail at a gaging station at the river's edge.

HETCH HETCHY
DOME
6,197'

Creek

RANCHERIA FALLS TRAIL

Tiltill

TO
RANCHERIA
FALLS

Rancheria Cr.

Hetch Hetchy Reservoir

KOLANA ROCK
5,772'

SMITH PEAK
7,751

WAPAMA FALLS
O'SHAUGHNESSY DAM
HIKES 22–23

Hike 24
Poopenaut Valley

Hiking distance: 3 miles round trip
Hiking time: 1.5 hours
Elevation gain: 1,250 feet
Maps: U.S.G.S. Lake Eleanor

Summary of hike: If you like to have the river all to yourself, this is the hike. Poopenaut Valley, a small, level valley once occupied by cattlemen and sheepherders, sits in the lower canyon of the Tuolumne River downstream from O'Shaughnessy Dam and the Hetch Hetchy Reservoir. The trail to Poopenaut Valley is a brutally steep path, discouraging most hikers. The trail does provide quick and rewarding access to an isolated pastoral area along the Tuolumne River. Watch for rattlesnakes.

Driving directions: From the Big Oak Flat entrance station on Highway 120, drive one mile west (outside the park) to Evergreen Road, the first turnoff on the right. Turn right and continue 7.4 miles to a T-junction at the end of the road. Turn right on Hetch Hetchy Road and drive 1.3 miles to the Hetch Hetchy entrance station. Enter the park and continue 3.9 miles to the posted trail sign on the left. Park in the pullout on the right.

Hiking directions: Cross the road to the signed trailhead, and descend from the Hetch Hetchy Road into the Yosemite Wilderness. The path starts out at a moderately level grade and quickly steepens. Drop into the shady pine, fir, cedar and oak forest, zigzagging down the mountainside. At one mile, the trail reaches a seasonal stream by a waterfall. Curve left and follow the stream to the valley floor. Stroll through the level valley, crossing a large grassy meadow rich with ferns. The path quickly reaches the Tuolumne River at a small beach pocket. Choose your own route up and down the river. At the lower end of the valley are beautiful rock-lined pools. Return along the same trail.

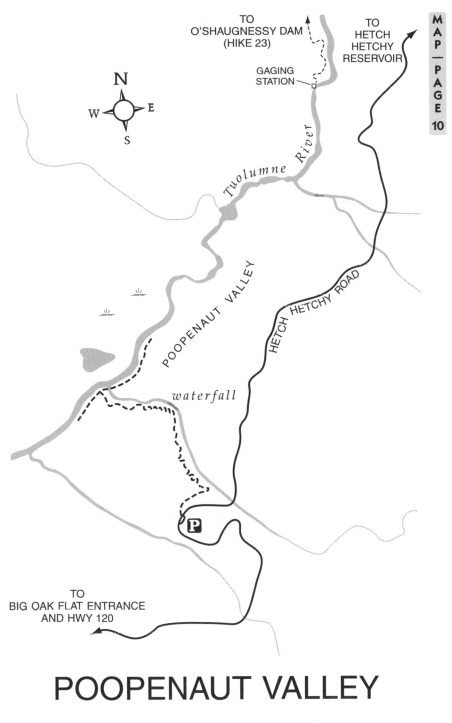

TO
O'SHAUGNESSY DAM
(HIKE 23)

TO
HETCH
HETCHY
RESERVOIR

GAGING
STATION

N

W   E

S

Tuolumne River

POOPENAUT VALLEY

HETCH HETCHY ROAD

waterfall

P

TO
BIG OAK FLAT ENTRANCE
AND HWY 120

POOPENAUT VALLEY

Hike 25
Lookout Point

Hiking distance: 2.7 miles round trip
Hiking time: 1.5 hours
Elevation gain: 500 feet
Maps: U.S.G.S. Lake Eleanor

Summary of hike: Lookout Point is on the crest of a barren, granite knoll with panoramic views of the lower Tuolumne River canyon, O'Shaughnessy Dam and the Hetch Hetchy Reservoir. Atop the 5,309-foot summit are a few scattered Jeffrey pines. The trail begins at the Mather Ranger Station by the Hetch Hetchy entrance to the park. Watch for rattlesnakes.

Driving directions: From the Big Oak Flat entrance station on Highway 120, drive one mile west (outside the park) to Evergreen Road, the first turnoff on the right. Turn right and continue 7.4 miles to a T-junction at the end of the road. Turn right on Hetch Hetchy Road, and drive 1.3 miles to the Hetch Hetchy entrance station. Enter the park and immediately park in the pullout on the right by the Mather Ranger Station.

Hiking directions: The posted trailhead is across the driveway from the Mather Ranger Station. Take the footpath through a small meadow, and enter a forest of ponderosa pine, incense cedar and black oak to a posted T-junction at 0.2 miles. The right fork leads to Cottonwood Meadow and Smith Peak. Take the left fork and parallel Hetch Hetchy Road, traversing the lupine covered hillside. After climbing up and over a small rise, curve right away from the road. Ascend a rocky slope to a plateau between two rocky mountains. In the spring, the plateau is lush with streams and wetlands. At one mile is a trail fork with a spur trail to Lookout Point. Bear left, passing a seasonal pond, and curve left. Leave the forest, climbing up the smooth glaciated knoll with stunted Jeffrey pines. From the rounded exposed summit are distant views of Tueeulala and Wapama Falls cascading into Hetch Hetchy Reservoir (Hike 22).

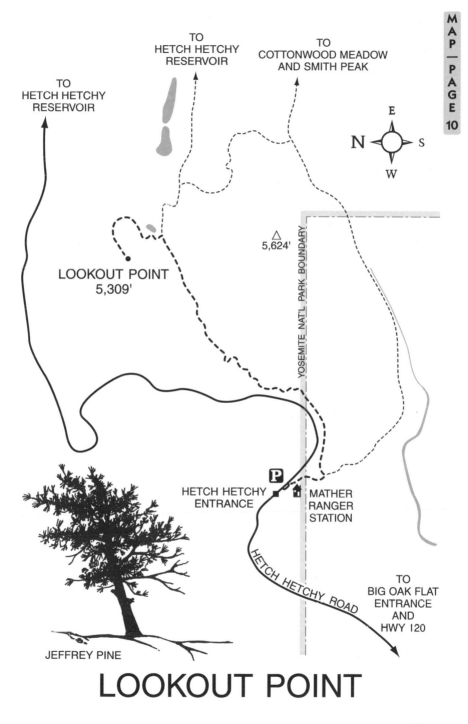

TO
HETCH HETCHY
RESERVOIR

TO
HETCH HETCHY
RESERVOIR

TO
COTTONWOOD MEADOW
AND SMITH PEAK

N E S W

△
5,624'

YOSEMITE NAT'L PARK BOUNDARY

LOOKOUT POINT
5,309'

P
HETCH HETCHY
ENTRANCE

MATHER
RANGER
STATION

HETCH HETCHY ROAD

TO
BIG OAK FLAT
ENTRANCE
AND
HWY 120

JEFFREY PINE

LOOKOUT POINT

Hike 26
Carlon Falls

Hiking distance: 3.6 miles round trip
Hiking time: 2 hours
Elevation gain: 200 feet
Maps: U.S.G.S. Ackerson Mountain

Summary of hike: Carlon Falls is a magnificent 35-foot cataract on the South Fork Tuolumne River. The waterfall cascades over wide granite ledges into a large pool surrounded by boulders. The falls was named after Donna Carlon, owner of a resort built in 1919 just inside the park boundary. The hike begins in the Stanislaus National Forest on the banks of the river and crosses into the western region of Yosemite National Park. The trail follows the north side of the river upstream to the pool and waterfall.

Driving directions: From the Big Oak Flat entrance station on Highway 120, drive one mile west (outside the park) to Evergreen Road, the first turnoff on the right. Turn right and continue one mile to the bridge crossing the South Fork Tuolumne River. Park immediately after crossing the bridge in the pullout on the right.

Hiking directions: Take the unsigned path along the north bank of the South Fork Tuolumne River. Head upstream through the lush forest of oak, cedar and pine. Enter the Yosemite National Park boundary at just under 0.2 miles, and cross over an old house foundation 100 yards ahead. The trail is not maintained, but it is distinct and follows an easy grade on a soft mat of pine needles. Cross over a few downfall trees on the undulating path. Pass a sandy beach pocket at a half mile, and continue through an understory of ferns. At 1.6 miles, the path climbs up an eroded hillside to the ridge. Gradually descend on the winding path to the river at a left river bend. Cascades and small waterfalls tumble over large, flat rock slabs. The path soon ends by huge, smooth boulders at Carlon Falls.

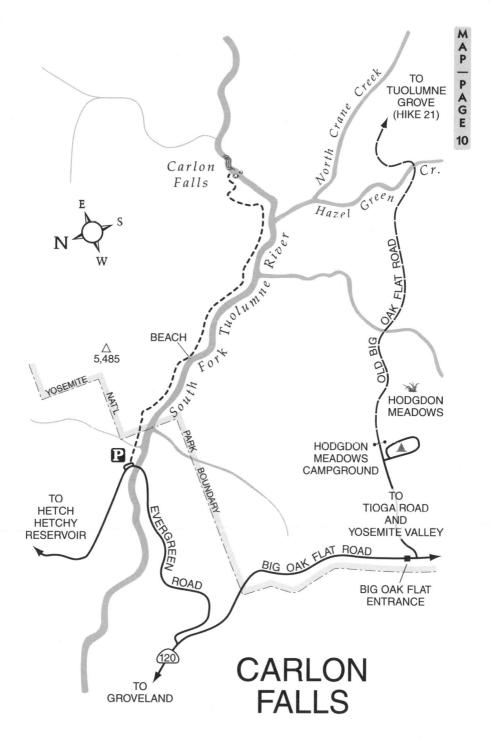

TO TUOLUMNE GROVE (HIKE 21)

North Crane Creek

Carlon Falls

Hazel Green Cr.

OLD BIG OAK FLAT ROAD

E
N — S
W

South Fork Tuolumne River

BEACH

△ 5,485

YOSEMITE NAT'L PARK BOUNDARY

HODGDON MEADOWS

HODGDON MEADOWS CAMPGROUND

P

TO HETCH HETCHY RESERVOIR

EVERGREEN ROAD

TO TIOGA ROAD AND YOSEMITE VALLEY

BIG OAK FLAT ROAD

BIG OAK FLAT ENTRANCE

120

TO GROVELAND

CARLON FALLS

Hike 27
Merced Grove of Giant Sequoias

Hiking distance: 4 miles round trip
Hiking time: 2 hours
Elevation gain: 400 feet
Maps: U.S.G.S. Ackerson Mountain and El Portal

Summary of hike: Yosemite has three giant sequoia groves. Merced Grove is the smallest and least visited. It is a dense, natural forest uninterrupted by development. About twenty giant sequoias are scattered within a mixed forest of white fir, incense cedar, ponderosa pine and sugar pine. The Russell Cabin (also called Merced Grove Cabin) is an old ranger station that rests in the shady grove. A stream runs through the forest in the canyon. This is not a populated trail, so you will have an opportunity to enjoy a quiet and secluded tour of these magnificent trees.

Driving directions: From the Highway 120/140 junction at the west end of Yosemite Valley, take Highway 120 for 13.3 miles to the signed Merced Grove parking lot on the left, located 3.5 miles past the Crane Flat Campground.
From the Tioga Road turnoff, drive 3.7 miles west on Highway 120 to the Merced Grove parking lot on the left.

Hiking directions: From the parking lot, head south through a beautifully forested area along an old gravel fire road. At 0.75 miles is a trail fork. Take the left fork and pass the gate. For the next mile the trail descends along the curving road to the canyon floor. At the bottom of the hill, the trail curves to the left. At this curve are six giant sequoias. From here, sequoias are sprinkled throughout the forest. The boarded-up Russell Cabin sits in the grove to the right. Several side trails lead down to the stream and past more giant sequoias. Although the trail continues down canyon, this is our turnaround spot. Return along the same route.

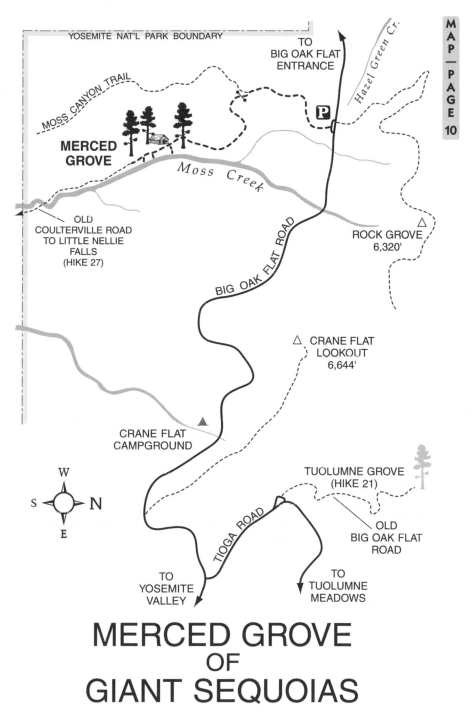

YOSEMITE NAT'L PARK BOUNDARY

TO
BIG OAK FLAT
ENTRANCE

Hazel Green Cr.

MOSS CANYON TRAIL

P

**MERCED
GROVE**

Moss   Creek

OLD
COULTERVILLE ROAD
TO LITTLE NELLIE
FALLS
(HIKE 27)

△
ROCK GROVE
6,320'

BIG OAK FLAT ROAD

△ CRANE FLAT
LOOKOUT
6,644'

CRANE FLAT
CAMPGROUND

TUOLUMNE GROVE
(HIKE 21)

OLD
BIG OAK FLAT
ROAD

W
S ✛ N
E

TIOGA ROAD

TO
YOSEMITE
VALLEY

TO
TUOLUMNE
MEADOWS

MERCED GROVE
OF
GIANT SEQUOIAS

Hike 28
Little Nellie Falls

Hiking distance: 5.6 miles round trip
Hiking time: 3 hours
Elevation gain: 600 feet
Maps: U.S.G.S. El Capitan and El Portal

Summary of hike: Little Nellie Falls is a 30-foot, two-tiered cataract cascading off moss-covered granite into a pool. The trail follows the Old Coulterville Road from Big Meadow to Little Nellie Falls just outside of the park in the Stanislaus National Forest. The Old Coulterville Road was the first wagon road extending into Yosemite Valley, dating back to 1874. A landslide permanently blocked the road in 1982.

Driving directions: From the Highway 120/140 junction at the west end of Yosemite Valley, take Highway 120 for 3.4 miles to the signed Foresta turnoff. Turn left and continue 1.8 miles to a turnout on the right by a forest service information board and a gated road. Park in the turnout on the right.

Hiking directions: Walk past the road gate, and follow the Old Coulterville Road past privately owned cabins. Curve around the west end of Big Meadow, and cross an old wooden bridge over Crane Creek. Curve right and head up the hillside on the open terrain to views of El Capitan and Half Dome in Yosemite Valley. At 0.8 miles is an unmarked road fork. Stay to the right and continue uphill. Pass a road gate, and drop into the shade of a conifer forest and a road split. Take the left fork and curve west on the winding road. Cross the hillside above the deep Little Crane Creek valley with views of Eagle Peak to the south and Buena Vista to the west. Enter a lush woodland of oak, cypress and pine, and wind 200 feet downhill to the park boundary at a trail gate. Cross into Stanislaus National Forest. At a quarter mile, the trail crosses Little Crane Creek. Upstream is Little Nellie Falls. Across the creek and downstream is a shady campsite and bench on a flat overlook of the creek.

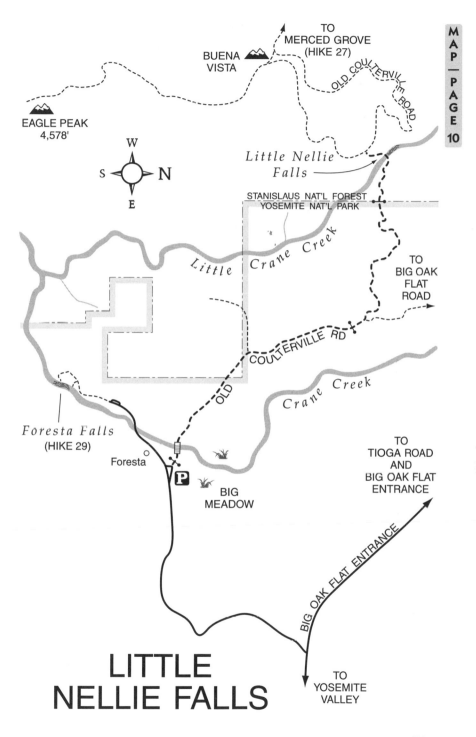

TO
MERCED GROVE
(HIKE 27)

BUENA
VISTA

OLD COULTERVILLE ROAD

EAGLE PEAK
4,578'

*Little Nellie
Falls*

STANISLAUS NAT'L FOREST
YOSEMITE NAT'L PARK

Little Crane Creek

TO
BIG OAK
FLAT
ROAD

OLD COULTERVILLE RD

Crane Creek

Foresta Falls
(HIKE 29)

Foresta

P

BIG
MEADOW

TO
TIOGA ROAD
AND
BIG OAK FLAT
ENTRANCE

BIG OAK FLAT ENTRANCE

LITTLE
NELLIE FALLS

TO
YOSEMITE
VALLEY

Hike 29
Foresta Falls

Hiking distance: 1 mile round trip
Hiking time: 30 minutes
Elevation gain: 200 feet
Maps: U.S.G.S. El Portal

Summary of hike: The town of Foresta is a small settlement tucked into a valley near Big Meadow. The valley is below Big Oak Flat Road just inside the boundary of Yosemite National Park. The hike follows an unpaved road a short distance along Crane Creek to Foresta Falls. The waterfall, which extends several hundred feet, is a long series of cascades and pools that drop over granite slabs.

Driving directions: From the Highway 120/140 junction at the west end of Yosemite Valley, take Highway 120 for 3.4 miles to the signed Foresta turnoff. Turn left and continue 2.4 miles to the end of the paved road. Park in the pullout on the right.

Hiking directions: Walk south down the unpaved road parallel to Crane Creek. Descend through an open pine forest in a scorched area from the 1990 fire that burned over 17,000 acres. A side path by five distinct boulders descends to large slab rocks at the creekside. Continue downhill on the main trail. Look back upstream to see Foresta Falls. On the left several faint paths scramble down the hill to the waterfall and overlooks of the falls. Return by following the same road back.

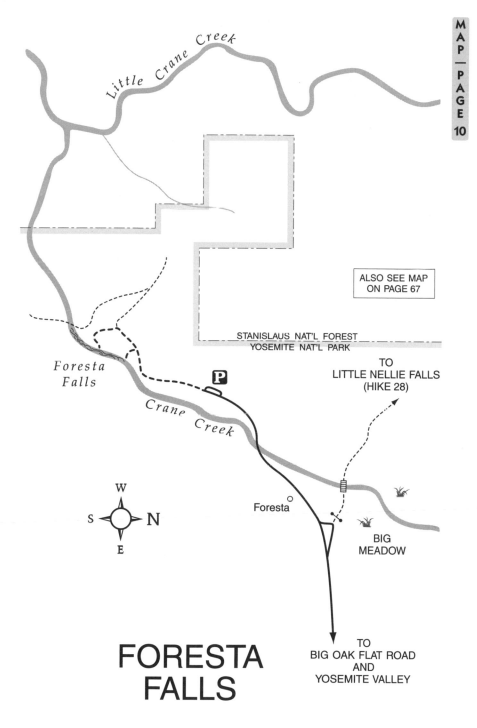

Little Crane Creek

ALSO SEE MAP
ON PAGE 67

STANISLAUS NAT'L FOREST
YOSEMITE NAT'L PARK

Foresta
Falls

Crane Creek

🅿

TO
LITTLE NELLIE FALLS
(HIKE 28)

W

S ✦ N

E

Foresta

BIG
MEADOW

FORESTA FALLS

TO
BIG OAK FLAT ROAD
AND
YOSEMITE VALLEY

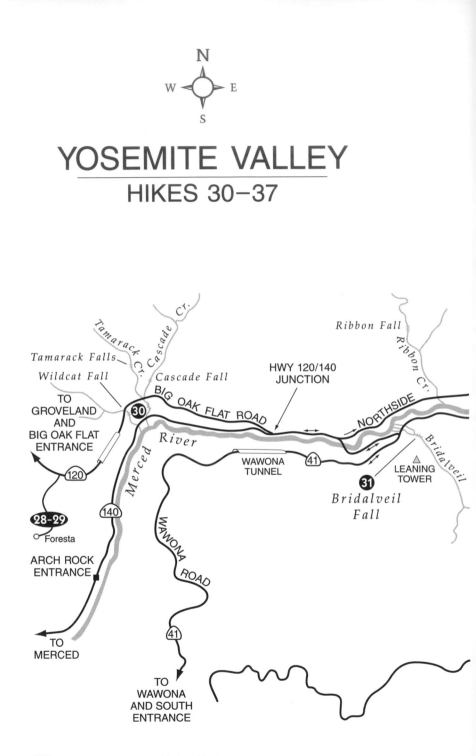

YOSEMITE VALLEY
HIKES 30–37

N
W E
S

Ribbon Fall
Ribbon Cr.

Tamarack Cr.
Cascade Cr.
Tamarack Falls
Wildcat Fall
Cascade Fall

HWY 120/140
JUNCTION

BIG OAK FLAT ROAD

NORTHSIDE

TO
GROVELAND
AND
BIG OAK FLAT
ENTRANCE

30

Merced River

Bridalveil

WAWONA
TUNNEL

41

LEANING
TOWER

31

Bridalveil
Fall

120

140

28-29
Foresta

ARCH ROCK
ENTRANCE

WAWONA

ROAD

41

TO
MERCED

TO
WAWONA
AND SOUTH
ENTRANCE

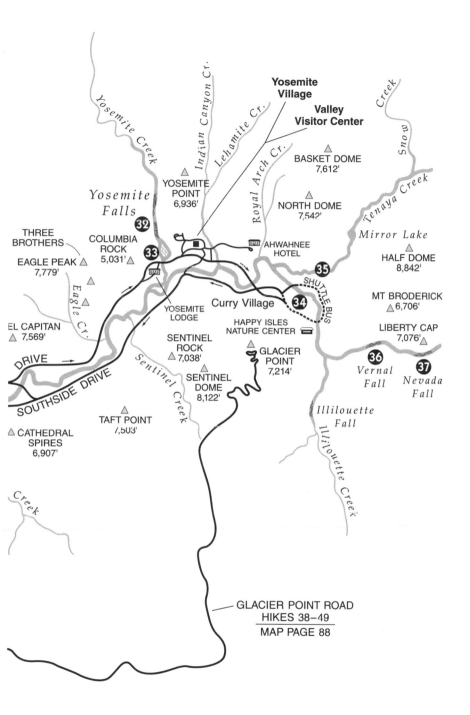

Yosemite Creek

Indian Canyon Cr.

Lehamite Cr.

Yosemite Village

Valley Visitor Center

Royal Arch Cr.

Snow Creek

BASKET DOME
7,612'

Yosemite Falls

YOSEMITE POINT
6,936'

NORTH DOME
7,542'

Tenaya Creek

Mirror Lake

THREE BROTHERS

32

COLUMBIA ROCK
5,031'

HALF DOME
8,842'

EAGLE PEAK
7,779'

33

AHWAHNEE HOTEL

35

Eagle Cr.

EL CAPITAN
7,569'

YOSEMITE LODGE

Curry Village

SHUTTLE BUS

34

MT BRODERICK
6,706'

DRIVE

SOUTHSIDE DRIVE

Sentinel Creek

SENTINEL ROCK
7,038'

HAPPY ISLES NATURE CENTER

GLACIER POINT
7,214'

LIBERTY CAP
7,076'

36

Vernal Fall

37

Nevada Fall

SENTINEL DOME
8,122'

CATHEDRAL SPIRES
6,907'

TAFT POINT
7,503'

Illilouette Fall

Illilouette Creek

Creek

GLACIER POINT ROAD
HIKES 38–49
MAP PAGE 88

Hike 30
The Cascades and Wildcat Falls

Hiking distance: 0.6 miles round trip
Hiking time: 30 minutes
Elevation gain: 50 feet
Maps: U.S.G.S. El Capitan

Summary of hike: The Cascades are located just below the confluence of Tamarack Creek and Cascade Creek. The watercourse tumbles 500 feet down the sloping canyon wall and empties into the Merced River. Wildcat Falls is a tall, narrow, freefalling cataract on Wildcat Creek that drops off a solid wall of granite rock. Both waterfalls are dramatically different in size and appearance. Short paths lead to the base of the waterfalls.

Driving directions: From the Highway 120/140 junction at the west end of Yosemite Valley, take Highway 140 (the south fork) for 1.7 miles, following the Merced River to the signed Cascade Falls parking area on the right.

Hiking directions: Begin at the interpretive panels and the overlook of The Cascades. Take the footpath parallel to Cascade Creek. The trail, which includes some boulder scrambling, passes numerous cascades and small waterfalls between the two forks of the creek. After picking your way upstream, return to the parking area.

To go to Wildcat Falls, parallel the road west to Wildcat Creek. Follow the creek upstream through the trees to the trail's end at the base of Wildcat Falls. For views of upper Wildcat Falls, return to the road and cross to the west side of the creek.

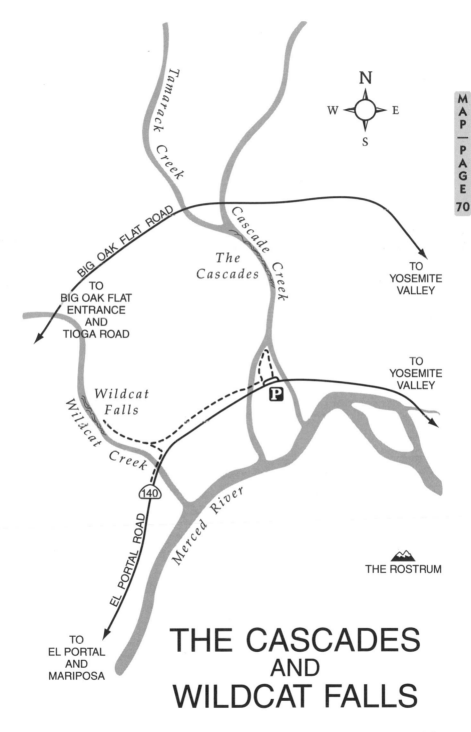

N

W · E

S

Tamarack Creek

BIG OAK FLAT ROAD

Cascade Creek

The Cascades

TO
YOSEMITE
VALLEY

TO
BIG OAK FLAT
ENTRANCE
AND
TIOGA ROAD

TO
YOSEMITE
VALLEY

Wildcat Falls

Wildcat Creek

P

140

EL PORTAL ROAD

Merced River

THE ROSTRUM

TO
EL PORTAL
AND
MARIPOSA

THE CASCADES
AND
WILDCAT FALLS

Hike 31
Bridalveil Fall

Hiking distance: 1.2 miles round trip
Hiking time: 45 minutes
Elevation gain: 100 feet
Maps: U.S.G.S. El Capitan

Summary of hike: Bridalveil Fall is a misty, free-falling water-fall resembling a veil when it is blown by the breezes. Its ribbon of water drops 620 feet off a vertical cliff from the "hanging valley" above to the boulders below on the southern wall of Yosemite Valley. The long fall plunges between Cathedral Rocks and Leaning Tower. This short, one-mile hike leads to Vista Point, a viewing area with a log bench near the base of Bridalveil Fall. The hike continues across three stone bridges over the branches of Bridalveil Creek to a view of the towering El Capitan across the valley floor.

Driving directions: At the west end of Yosemite Valley, the Bridalveil Fall parking lot is located on Wawona Road/Highway 41, 100 feet south of the intersection of Highway 41 and Southside Drive.

Hiking directions: The wide, paved hiking trail begins at the east end of the parking lot. Follow the trail about 200 feet to a signed trail fork. Take the trail to the right, leading gently uphill alongside Bridalveil Creek to Vista Point. A boulder field separates Vista Point from the base of the falls.

After viewing the falls from Vista Point, head back to the junction. Instead of returning to the parking lot, continue to the right. Cross the three stone bridges over Bridalveil Creek under a canopy of maple, oak, cedar and bay trees. The trail curves left to a trail junction a short distance before reaching Southside Drive, the road which loops through the valley. At the trail junction is a picture-perfect view of El Capitan on the north wall of the valley. Return along the same path.

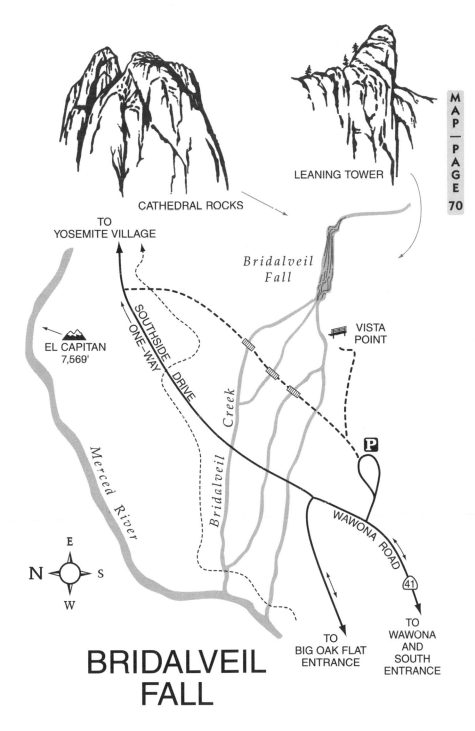

LEANING TOWER

CATHEDRAL ROCKS

TO
YOSEMITE VILLAGE

*Bridalveil
Fall*

SOUTHSIDE
ONE—WAY
DRIVE

EL CAPITAN
7,569'

VISTA
POINT

Merced River

Bridalveil Creek

P

WAWONA ROAD

E
N · S
W

41

TO
BIG OAK FLAT
ENTRANCE

TO
WAWONA
AND
SOUTH
ENTRANCE

BRIDALVEIL
FALL

Hike 32
Upper Yosemite Fall

Hiking distance: 7.2 miles round trip
Hiking time: 6 hours
Elevation gain: 2,700 feet
Maps: U.S.G.S. Half Dome and Yosemite Falls

Summary of hike: Yosemite Falls is the tallest waterfall in North America and fifth highest in the world, dropping 2,425 feet. The Upper Fall plummets 1,430 feet to the middle cascade. The cascade tumbles another 675 feet to the Lower Fall, which plunges 320 feet to the valley floor. The Yosemite Falls Trail is one of the park's oldest trails, built in the 1870s. It is a strenuous and challenging hike—leading from the valley floor, up the sheer north wall, to the precipice of Yosemite Falls on the upper plateau. The trail gains 2,700 feet in elevation.

Driving directions: Park in the lot at Yosemite Lodge.

Hiking directions: Cross Northside Drive and walk straight ahead 100 yards to a wide sandy path. Bear left and head west towards Sunnyside Campground (Camp 4). At the trail split, stay to the right to the signed Upper Yosemite Fall Trail, just shy of the campground. Curve right and head up the rocky trail, winding through the shade of the oak forest. Approximately sixty short switchbacks zigzag one mile and a thousand feet up the mountain to a panoramic viewpoint at Columbia Rock. From there, head up the steep sandy slope, and follow a wooded ledge. The trail bends north to the first view of Upper Yosemite Fall. After a short descent, traverse the narrow side canyon with steady close-up views of the falls. Continue up the seemingly endless, tight, steep switchbacks to the plateau atop the valley's north wall, where the trail levels out. Reach a signed junction with the Eagle Peak Trail. Bear to the right (east) towards Yosemite Creek to a short spur trail on the right. The treacherous right fork leads down the cliff face past sculpted rocks and Jeffrey pines. Work your way down granite steps to a ledge and railing above Yosemite Creek with a vertiginous overlook of Yosemite Valley from the lip of the falls. Return to the main trail and continue east to Yosemite Creek at a wooden bridge. Cross the bridge and climb 0.8 miles to Yosemite Point for another awesome vista. Return along the same trail.

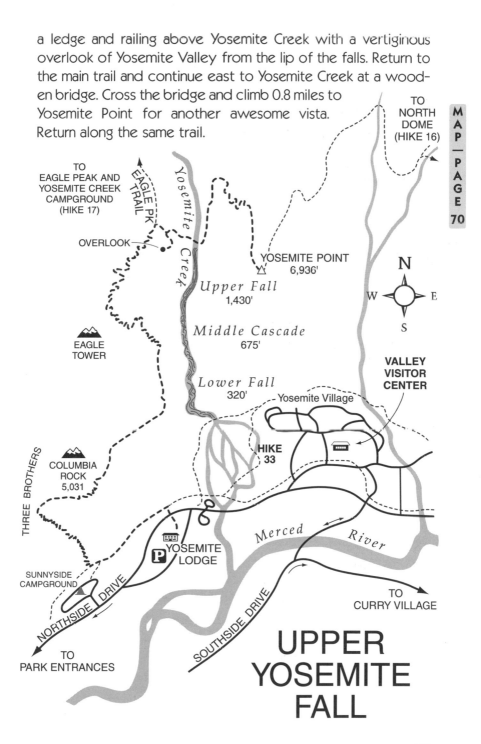

TO NORTH DOME (HIKE 16)

TO EAGLE PEAK AND YOSEMITE CREEK CAMPGROUND (HIKE 17)

EAGLE PK TRAIL

Yosemite Creek

OVERLOOK

YOSEMITE POINT 6,936'

Upper Fall 1,430'

N

W E

S

Middle Cascade 675'

EAGLE TOWER

VALLEY VISITOR CENTER

Lower Fall 320'

Yosemite Village

HIKE 33

COLUMBIA ROCK 5,031'

THREE BROTHERS

Merced River

YOSEMITE LODGE P

SUNNYSIDE CAMPGROUND

NORTHSIDE DRIVE

SOUTHSIDE DRIVE

TO CURRY VILLAGE

TO PARK ENTRANCES

UPPER YOSEMITE FALL

Hike 33
Lower Yosemite Fall

Hiking distance: 0.5 miles round trip from parking lot
1.5 miles round trip from visitor center
Hiking time: 20 to 45 minutes
Elevation gain: Level
Maps: U.S.G.S. Half Dome and Yosemite Falls

Summary of hike: This short and busy trail leads to the base of North America's tallest waterfall. The fall drops 2,425 feet, nearly a half mile, in three tiers from the steep granite cliffs. The paved, wheelchair-accessible trail leads to a bridge crossing Yosemite Creek and a viewing area of the 320-foot drop of Lower Yosemite Fall.

Driving directions: Park in the Yosemite Falls parking lot 0.5 miles west of the Yosemite Valley Visitor Center. If the lot is full, park across the road in the Yosemite Lodge parking lot. (By shuttle bus, this is Stop No. 7.) You may also walk from the Yosemite Valley Visitor Center for an enjoyable 1.5-mile round trip hike.

Hiking directions: From the Yosemite Falls parking lot, walk north on the paved trail, passing several interpretive panels. The long, narrow falls is framed by the tall ponderosa pines and incense cedars lining the path. At a quarter mile is a viewing area of the lower fall and a bridge that crosses the boulder-filled creekbed of Yosemite Creek. There are beautiful cascades among the boulders. You may return now or continue past the bridge along the base of the cliffs. After the bridge, stay to the right, crossing five small bridges over the divided creek. The short path loops back to the trailhead parking lot.

From the visitor center, take the bike path west to the Yosemite Falls parking lot, and continue north on the paved trail.

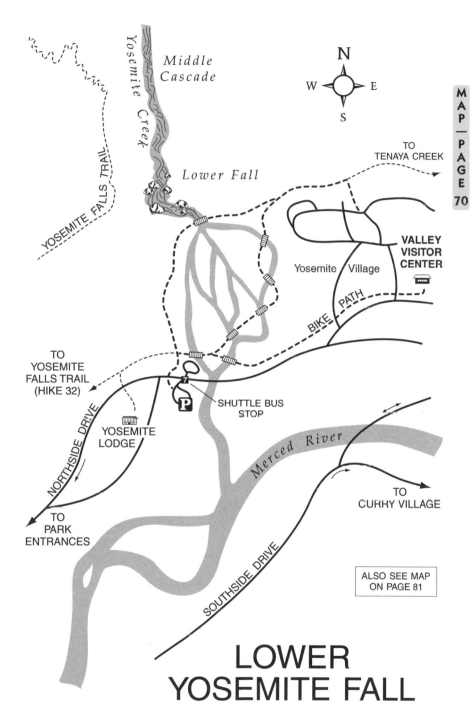

Yosemite Creek

Middle Cascade

N
W E
S

MAP—PAGE 70

TO TENAYA CREEK

Lower Fall

YOSEMITE FALLS TRAIL

VALLEY VISITOR CENTER

Yosemite Village

BIKE PATH

TO YOSEMITE FALLS TRAIL (HIKE 32)

SHUTTLE BUS STOP

NORTHSIDE DRIVE

YOSEMITE LODGE

P

Merced River

TO PARK ENTRANCES

TO CURRY VILLAGE

SOUTHSIDE DRIVE

ALSO SEE MAP ON PAGE 81

LOWER YOSEMITE FALL

Hike 34
East Valley Loop
along the Merced River

Hiking distance: 2.5 mile loop
Hiking time: 1.5 hours
Elevation gain: Level
Maps: U.S.G.S. Half Dome

Summary of hike: This valley loop trail is an easy, beautiful stroll at the east end of Yosemite Valley. The hike includes a visit to the Happy Isles Nature Center and the tumbling whitewater along the banks of the Merced River. The trail starts near Curry Village.

Driving directions: Park in the Curry Village parking lot or take the Yosemite Valley shuttle bus to Stop No. 14 or No. 15. The trail is to the south of the shuttle bus road.

Hiking directions: From the southeast corner of the Curry Village parking lot, take the footpath parallel to the shuttle bus road. Head east towards Happy Isles, passing the tent cabins on your right. Continue one mile through the shady incense and ponderosa pine forest to Happy Isles. Turn right towards the nature center. This is a good opportunity to enjoy the Happy Isles area and the center. To continue with the hike, cross the bridge over the Merced River. Take the trail to the left (north), and head downstream along the east bank of the river. (The trail to the right leads to Vernal and Nevada Falls, Hikes 36 and 37.) Continue along the river one mile, with views of North Dome and Upper Yosemite Fall, to the horse stables. Cross Clarks Bridge over the Merced River. The footpath soon passes the entrances to Upper and Lower Pines Campgrounds. Turn right at the shuttle bus road, heading towards Stoneman Meadow. This leads back to the Curry Village parking lot on the left.

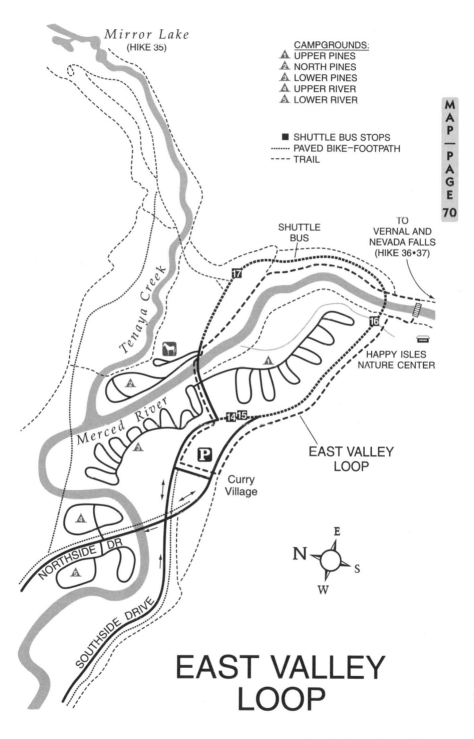

Mirror Lake
(HIKE 35)

CAMPGROUNDS:
🏕 UPPER PINES
🏕 NORTH PINES
🏕 LOWER PINES
🏕 UPPER RIVER
🏕 LOWER RIVER

■ SHUTTLE BUS STOPS
········· PAVED BIKE–FOOTPATH
– – – TRAIL

SHUTTLE
BUS

TO
VERNAL AND
NEVADA FALLS
(HIKE 36•37)

Tenaya Creek

17

16

HAPPY ISLES
NATURE CENTER

14 15

Merced River

EAST VALLEY
LOOP

P

Curry
Village

NORTHSIDE DR

SOUTHSIDE DRIVE

N
E
S
W

EAST VALLEY
LOOP

Hike 35
Mirror Lake and Tenaya Canyon

Hiking distance: 4.4 mile loop
Hiking time: 2 hours
Elevation gain: 200 feet
Maps: U.S.G.S. Half Dome and Yosemite Falls

Summary of hike: This hike follows Tenaya Creek up the glaciated Tenaya Canyon. The trail travels through a cedar, fir and oak tree forest. The hike includes a visit to Mirror Lake, which is evolving into Mirror Meadow. The tranquil lake on Tenaya Creek has filled in and has become a marshy area with a shallow pool of water and a sand bar beach. From the lake are magnificent views of Mount Watkins, Basket Dome, North Dome and one of Yosemite's premiere views of Half Dome.

Driving directions: The hike begins from the shuttle bus loop at the east end of Yosemite Valley. Take the free shuttle bus to Mirror Lake/Stop No. 17, or walk to the trailhead a quarter mile east of the stables at the end of the valley.

Hiking directions: The hike begins just before the Tenaya Bridge. Before crossing the stone bridge, take the footpath to the right and a quick left. Head upstream along the southeast side of Tenaya Creek. The trail gently climbs past massive, moss-covered boulders to the east shore of Mirror Lake at the base of Half Dome. Continue up canyon 2.1 miles to a bridge. From the bridge, the trail loops back along the northwest side of the creek. Continue 0.3 miles to the Snow Creek Trail, climbing out of Tenaya Canyon to North Dome and Tuolumne Meadows. Continue down canyon. Upon reaching the Mirror Lake meadow, there is an awesome view of Half Dome's 4,700-foot perpendicular face. Mirror Lake used to carry its reflection. From here you may take either the footpath or the asphalt pedestrian-only road. Both will lead back to the trailhead.

This trail is also used by horses, which adds an extra fragrance and a human-friendly assortment of flies.

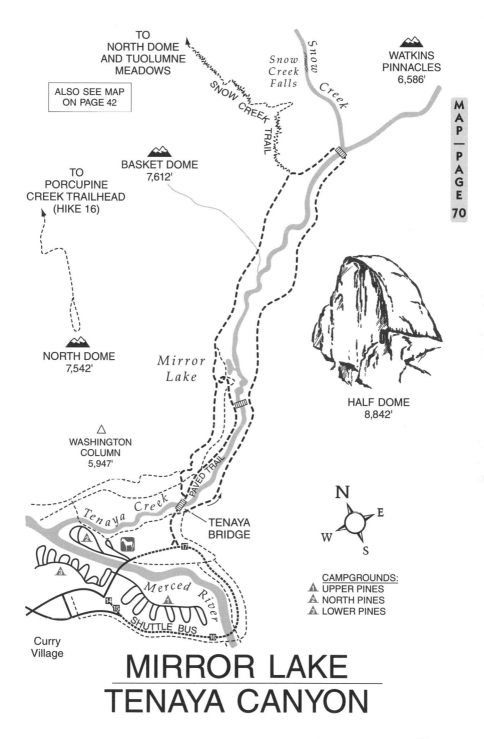

TO
NORTH DOME
AND TUOLUMNE
MEADOWS

ALSO SEE MAP
ON PAGE 42

*Snow
Creek
Falls*

Snow Creek

WATKINS
PINNACLES
6,586'

BASKET DOME
7,612'

TO
PORCUPINE
CREEK TRAILHEAD
(HIKE 16)

SNOW CREEK TRAIL

NORTH DOME
7,542'

*Mirror
Lake*

HALF DOME
8,842'

△
WASHINGTON
COLUMN
5,947'

PAVED TRAIL

Tenaya Creek

N
E
W
S

TENAYA
BRIDGE

CAMPGROUNDS:
△1 UPPER PINES
△2 NORTH PINES
△3 LOWER PINES

17

Merced River

△3

14
15

△

SHUTTLE BUS

16

Curry
Village

MIRROR LAKE
TENAYA CANYON

Hikes 36 and 37
Vernal Fall and Nevada Fall

Summary of the hikes: These two hikes head up the Merced River Canyon between Half Dome and Glacier Point among sheer granite walls, deep gorges and classic glacial features. The trail parallels the Merced River to the base and top of both Vernal Fall and Nevada Fall. These falls are part of Merced Canyon's "Giant Staircase." This glacial stairway plunges 317 feet at Vernal Fall and 594 feet at Nevada Fall. The trail to the falls climbs through the steep granite gorge with stunning views of these two world-class waterfalls, plus views of Glacier Point, Half Dome, Illilouette Fall and Upper Yosemite Fall. The hike crosses the Merced River four times via bridges. Along the Mist Trail, mist from the large volume of water plunging over Vernal Fall sprays the canyon walls that are carpeted with moss, ferns and deep green foliage. Early in the season, the mist also sprays the trail and hikers. Rain gear is recommended, or you will get soaked.

The trailhead is the start of the John Muir Trail. The John Muir Trail leads south to the summit of Mount Whitney, 212 miles away.

Caution: Do not swim in the pools above either waterfall. They may look safe and inviting, but they do contain strong currents. The consequences of going in could effect the rest of your vacation.

Driving directions for Hikes 36 and 37: From Yosemite Valley, take the free shuttle bus to the Happy Isles Nature Center/Stop No. 16 at the east end of the valley.

From Curry Village, walk one mile southeast along the footpath parallel to the shuttle bus road to the Happy Isles Nature Center. A map is on page 87.

Hike 36
Vernal Fall

Hiking distance: 3 miles round trip
Hiking time: 2.5 hours
Elevation gain: 1,000 feet
Maps: U.S.G.S. Half Dome

map
next page

Hiking directions: From the Happy Isles Nature Center, cross the bridge over the Merced River. The trail begins on a wide, paved path curving up canyon past enormous boulders. The Merced River rages downstream on your right. Across the canyon in a narrow gorge, Illilouette Fall can be seen as it plunges 370 feet over a vertical cliff from its hanging valley. At 0.8 miles, the Vernal Fall Bridge crosses the Merced River. From this bridge is a dramatic view up river of the 80-foot wide Vernal Fall plunging over the bold granite cliffs. Mount Broderick and the bell-shaped Liberty Cap loom above. Turn around here for a 1.6-mile round-trip hike.

To reach the top of Vernal Fall, continue uphill on the southern bank of the Merced River. A quarter mile past the bridge is a trail fork. Bear left, towards Vernal Fall, along the canyon's edge on the Mist Trail. (The John Muir Trail continues on the right fork to the top of Nevada Fall, the return trail of Hike 37.) The Mist Trail heads up a series of steep granite steps to the cliff face. You will feel the billowing mist and see rainbows from the powerful falls. Use caution, as the steps can be wet and slippery. At the top of Vernal Fall, large granite slabs and a railing lead down to the brink. Then, follow the river upstream a short distance to Silver Apron, a 200-foot cascade sliding over smooth rocks into the green water of Emerald Pool. This is an excellent area to relax and enjoy a rest as a reward for the climb. Swimming in Emerald Pool is discouraged, as it could be very uncomfortable going over Vernal Fall.

To hike to the top of Nevada Fall, continue with the next hike. If not, return along the same trail. An alternative return route is on a loop via Clark Point, following a half-mile trail up a series of switchbacks to the John Muir Trail. At Clark Point, proceed to the right, heading back to the Mist Trail. Cross the Vernal Fall Bridge and return to the nature center.

Hike 37
Nevada Fall

Hiking distance: 6 miles round trip (total of Hikes 36 & 37)
Hiking time: 5 hours
Elevation gain: 1,900 feet
Maps: U.S.G.S. Half Dome

Hiking directions: From the top of Vernal Fall and Silver Apron—where Hike 36 left off—hike upstream to a bridge, and cross the Merced River to the north side of the canyon. The trail to the top of Nevada Fall, at the head of the canyon, gains 900 feet in 0.9 miles via switchbacks and granite steps. Near the top, the trail curves along the base of Liberty Cap to a junction. The right fork leads down to the falls. (The left fork leads to Little Yosemite Valley and Half Dome, a popular overnight trip.) At Nevada Fall, just before the bridge, a side trail leads to a spectacular observation platform and railed terrace at the brink of the falls. To return, follow the same trail back or make a loop via the John Muir Trail.

To return along the John Muir Trail, cross the bridge over the Merced River above the waterfall's chute to the south canyon wall. Within minutes is a trail junction. Stay to the right, continuing along the John Muir Trail. (The Panorama Trail to the left leads to Illilouette Fall and Glacier Point, Hikes 48 and 49.) From the south wall of the Merced Gorge are magnificent views of Half Dome, Mount Broderick and Liberty Cap towering above Nevada Fall. Continue downhill one mile to another trail junction at Clark Point. The right fork zigzags downhill 0.4 miles and rejoins the Mist Trail. The left fork continues on the John Muir Trail below Panorama Cliff. Both routes join at the Vernal Fall Bridge. Cross the bridge and return 0.8 miles to the nature center.

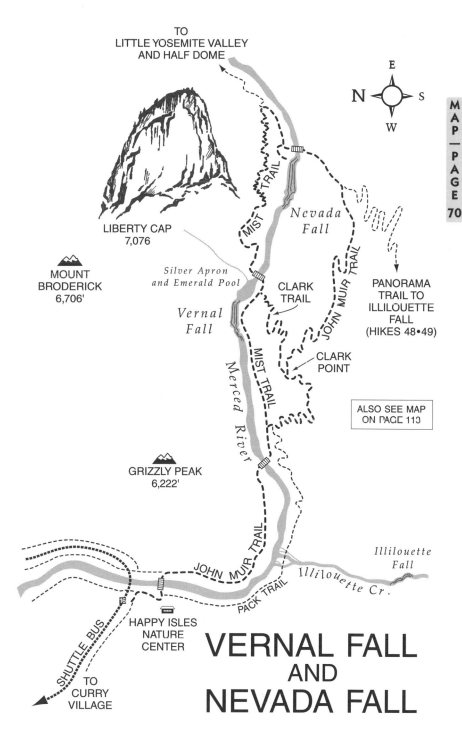

TO
LITTLE YOSEMITE VALLEY
AND HALF DOME

N E S W

M
A
P
—
P
A
G
E
70

LIBERTY CAP
7,076'

*Nevada
Fall*

MIST TRAIL

MOUNT
BRODERICK
6,706'

*Silver Apron
and Emerald Pool*

CLARK
TRAIL

JOHN MUIR TRAIL

PANORAMA
TRAIL TO
ILLILOUETTE
FALL
(HIKES 48•49)

*Vernal
Fall*

CLARK
POINT

MIST TRAIL

Merced River

ALSO SEE MAP
ON PAGE 113

GRIZZLY PEAK
6,222'

JOHN MUIR TRAIL

*Illilouette
Fall*

JOHN MUIR TRAIL

Illilouette Cr.

PACK TRAIL

16

SHUTTLE BUS

HAPPY ISLES
NATURE
CENTER

TO
CURRY
VILLAGE

VERNAL FALL
AND
NEVADA FALL

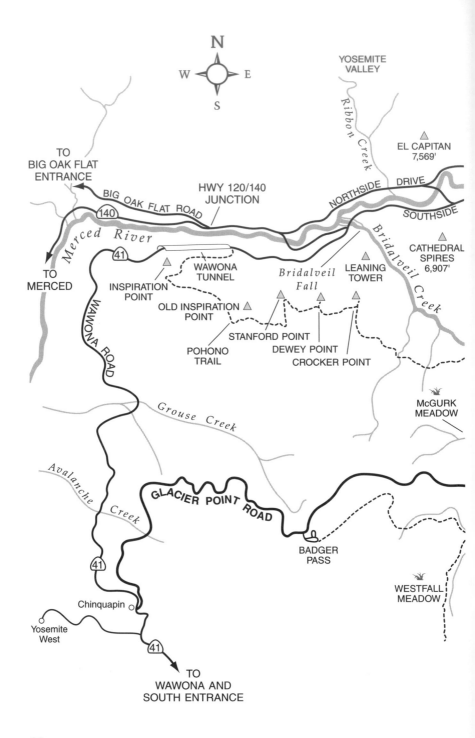

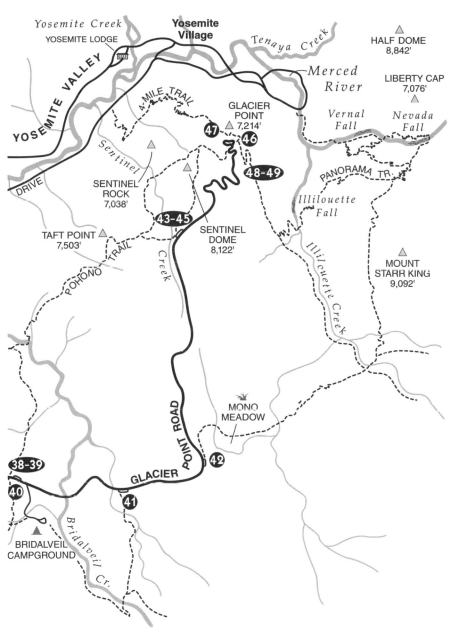

GLACIER POINT ROAD
HIKES 38–49

Hike 38
McGurk Meadow

Hiking distance: 3.8 miles round trip
Hiking time: 2 hours
Elevation gain: 200 feet
Maps: U.S.G.S. El Capitan and Half Dome

Summary of hike: McGurk Meadow is a pristine, mile-long meadow with a tributary of Bridalveil Creek meandering through its center. The McGurk Meadow Trail leads downhill through a fir and pine forest to the stream-fed meadow. At the edge of the meadow is an old pioneer cabin built in the 1890s by John McGurk, who used it as a summer home while grazing sheep.

Driving directions: From the west end of Yosemite Valley, drive 9 miles south on Wawona Road/Highway 41 to Glacier Point Road. Turn left (east) and continue 7.6 miles to the parking pullout on the left, 70 yards past the signed trailhead on the left. The pullout is 0.1 mile west of the Bridalveil Campground.

Hiking directions: Return 70 yards west on Glacier Point Road to the posted McGurk Meadow Trail on the right. Take the footpath north into the lodgepole pine forest, and meander on a gentle downslope grade. Pass John McGurk's old log cabin on the left side of the trail at 0.7 miles. A hundred yards ahead emerge from the forest into McGurk Meadow. Cross a wooden footbridge over the small stream that snakes through the grassy meadow. Skirt the west edge of the meadow, tucked inside the treeline. Reenter the forest beyond McGurk Meadow, and gradually descend to a Y-fork with the Pohono Trail at 1.9 miles. This is our turnaround spot.

The Pohono Trail travels along the south rim of Yosemite Valley for 13 miles from Taft and Glacier Points in the east to Dewey, Crocker, Stanford and Inspiration Points in the west. To hike to Dewey and Crocker Points continue with the next hike.

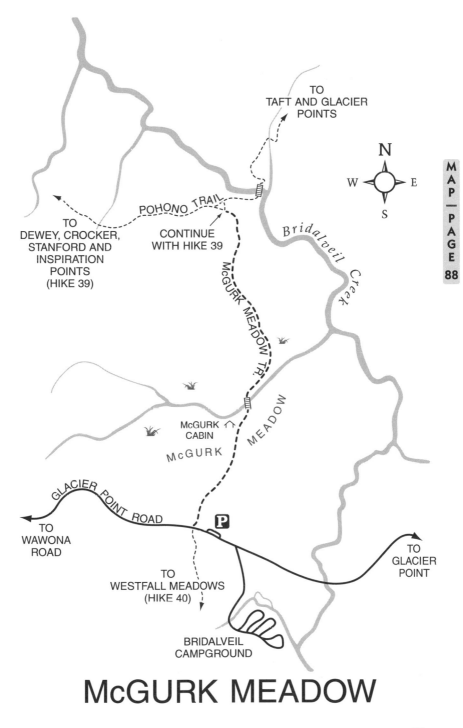

TO
TAFT AND GLACIER
POINTS

N
W E
S

POHONO TRAIL

Bridalveil Creek

TO
DEWEY, CROCKER,
STANFORD AND
INSPIRATION
POINTS
(HIKE 39)

CONTINUE
WITH HIKE 39

McGURK MEADOW TR.

MEADOW

McGURK
CABIN

McGURK

GLACIER POINT ROAD

P

TO
WAWONA
ROAD

TO
GLACIER
POINT

TO
WESTFALL MEADOWS
(HIKE 40)

BRIDALVEIL
CAMPGROUND

McGURK MEADOW

Hike 39
Dewey Point and Crocker Point
Pohono Trail

Hiking distance: 7.8—9.2 miles round trip
Hiking time: 4 hours
Elevation gain: 400 feet
Maps: U.S.G.S. El Capitan and Half Dome

Summary of hike: Dewey Point and Crocker Point are two overlooks perched on the south rim of Yosemite Valley, 3,500 feet and 3,100 feet above the valley floor. From the overlooks are sweeping birds-eye views of the entire valley, including Tenaya Canyon, Half Dome, Clouds Rest, Cathedral Rocks, Cathedral Spires, Leaning Tower, Bridalveil Fall, Cascade Fall, Yosemite Falls, Three Brothers, El Capitan and Mount Hoffman.

Driving directions: Same as McGurk Meadow, Hike 38.

Hiking directions: Follow the hiking directions for Hike 38 to the McGurk Meadow Trail and Pohono Trail junction. To the right, the Pohono Trail leads to Taft Point and Glacier Point. Take the Pohono Trail to the left, and head west through the forest. Cross a tributary stream of Bridalveil Creek and ascend a hill, crossing a second feeder stream. Steadily climb through an old growth forest to a clearing near the ridge where the trail levels out. Views open up beyond Glacier Point to the Merced River canyon and across Yosemite Valley to the north rim. The path reaches Dewey Point by a deep cleft. To the right, a path leads out on the rock shelf point. To continue to Crocker Point, bear left and follow the edge of the 3,000-foot cliffs, marveling at the staggering views. Climb the hill through a pine grove, back from the cliff's edge. Descend to Crocker Point on a rocky flat that extends out on an overhanging cliff. This is our turnaround point.

To hike further, the Pohono Trail continues to Stanford Point, 0.7 miles ahead; Inspiration Point, 5.2 miles ahead; and down to the valley floor at the Wawona Tunnel, 7.8 miles ahead.

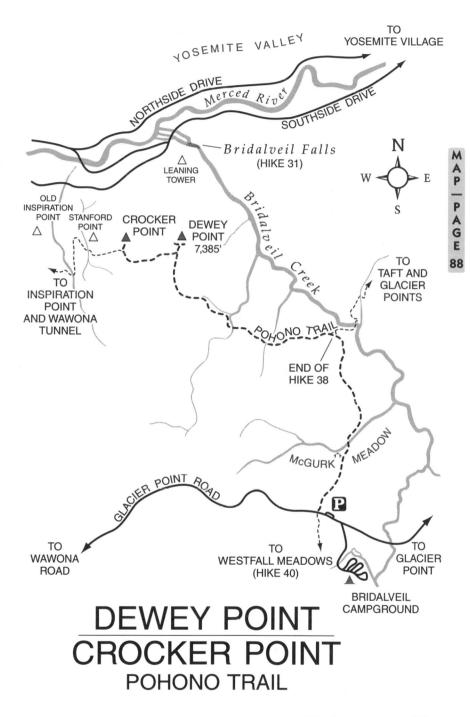

YOSEMITE VALLEY

TO YOSEMITE VILLAGE

NORTHSIDE DRIVE

Merced River

SOUTHSIDE DRIVE

Bridalveil Falls
(HIKE 31)

LEANING TOWER

N
W — E
S

MAP — PAGE 88

Bridalveil Creek

OLD INSPIRATION POINT

STANFORD POINT

CROCKER POINT

DEWEY POINT 7,385'

TO INSPIRATION POINT AND WAWONA TUNNEL

TO TAFT AND GLACIER POINTS

POHONO TRAIL

END OF HIKE 38

McGURK MEADOW

GLACIER POINT ROAD

P

TO WAWONA ROAD

TO WESTFALL MEADOWS (HIKE 40)

TO GLACIER POINT

BRIDALVEIL CAMPGROUND

DEWEY POINT
CROCKER POINT
POHONO TRAIL

Fifty-five Great Hikes - **93**

Hike 40
Westfall Meadows

Hiking distance: 3.4 miles round trip
Hiking time: 1.5 hours
Elevation gain: 200 feet
Maps: U.S.G.S. El Capitan

Summary of hike: Westfall Meadows is a half-mile-long meadow surrounded by pines. The trail follows a gentle grade through the forest, away from Yosemite's summer crowds. The meadow, a short distance from Bridalveil Campground, is wet during the spring and early summer. The stream draining the meadow flows through the campground before merging with Bridalveil Creek.

Driving directions: From the west end of Yosemite Valley, drive 9 miles south on Wawona Road/Highway 41 to Glacier Point Road. Turn left (east) and continue 7.6 miles to the parking pullout on the left, 70 yards past the signed McGurk Meadow trailhead on the left. The pullout is 0.1 mile west of the Bridalveil Campground. The Westfall Meadows Trail is directly across the road from the McGurk Meadow Trail.

Hiking directions: Return 70 yards west on Glacier Point Road to the posted McGurk Meadow Trail on the right. Cross the road to the unsigned but distinct trail. Head south into the Yosemite Wilderness at a trail sign. Follow the level path through an open pine forest, and gradually descend across large granite slabs and boulders. Cross a tributary stream of Bridalveil Creek. Parallel the stream, skirting the west side of a meadow to an old road crossing the trail. To the left, the road leads to Bridalveil Campground. Continue south on the footpath, winding through the forest above the drainage stream from Westfall Meadows. Emerge from the forest at Westfall Meadows, a large grassy meadow rimmed with pines. The open expanse is marbled with waterways. Early in the season, the meadow is marshy. A faint path crosses through the center of the meadow to the hills in the south. This is our turn-around spot.

To hike further, the trail continues to Deer Camp 3.5 miles ahead and follows Alder Creek to Alder Falls en route to Wawona, 11.5 miles ahead.

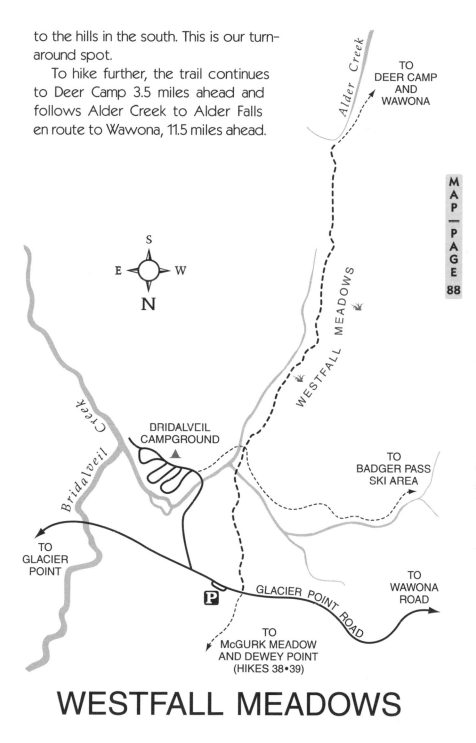

TO DEER CAMP AND WAWONA

Alder Creek

S

E ✦ W

N

WESTFALL MEADOWS

Bridalveil Creek

BRIDALVEIL CAMPGROUND

TO BADGER PASS SKI AREA

TO GLACIER POINT

P

GLACIER POINT ROAD

TO WAWONA ROAD

TO McGURK MEADOW AND DEWEY POINT (HIKES 38•39)

WESTFALL MEADOWS

Hike 41
Bridalveil Creek

Hiking distance: 5.5—7 miles round trip
Hiking time: 3 hours
Elevation gain: Near level
Maps: U.S.G.S. Half Dome

Summary of hike: This level trail parallels Bridalveil Creek through lodgepole pine forests and meadows. It is a quiet, away-from-the-crowds hike. Wildflowers are abundant along the meadows and the two creek crossings. The trail is also a popular cross-country ski trail during the winter that leads to a hut at Ostrander Lake. Two miles downstream from this hike, Bridalveil Creek produces Bridalveil Fall, dropping 620 feet off the southern wall of Yosemite Valley.

Driving directions: From the west end of Yosemite Valley, drive 9 miles south on Wawona Road/Highway 41 to Glacier Point Road. Turn left (east) and continue 9.1 miles to the Ostrander Lake Trail parking pullout on the right. The posted pullout is 1.3 miles past the Bridalveil Campground.

Hiking directions: From the Ostrander Lake Trailhead, walk south through the lodgepole pine forest on level terrain. At 0.2 miles, a wooden footbridge crosses a tributary of Bridalveil Creek. Continue 1.4 miles through the regenerating forest and meadow to a trail junction. Take the right fork leading to the Bridalveil Creek Campground. (The left fork heads to Ostrander Lake, 4.5 miles ahead.) The trail descends and crosses Bridalveil Creek in less than a quarter mile, using boulders as stepping stones. A short distance past the creek is another junction. Again, take the right fork. The trail parallels Bridalveil Creek to the campground, 1.7 miles from the junction. To return, you may follow the same trail back, or walk 1.3 miles east on Glacier Point Road.

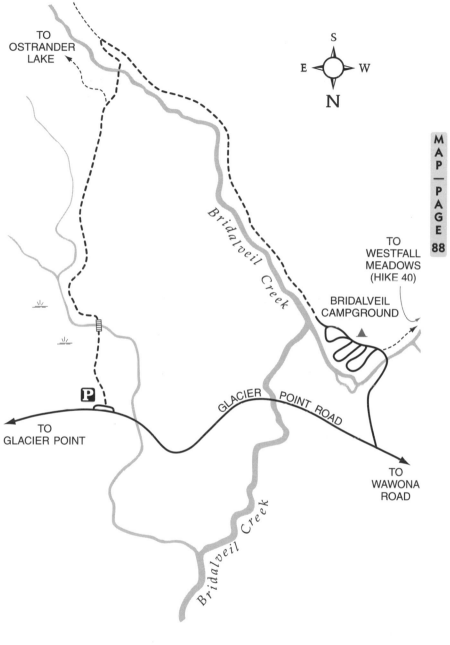

TO
OSTRANDER
LAKE

S
E W
N

Bridalveil Creek

TO
WESTFALL
MEADOWS
(HIKE 40)

BRIDALVEIL
CAMPGROUND

P

GLACIER POINT ROAD

TO
GLACIER POINT

TO
WAWONA
ROAD

Bridalveil Creek

Bridalveil Creek

BRIDALVEIL CREEK

Hike 42
Mono Meadow to overlook

Hiking distance: 3.5 miles round trip
Hiking time: 2 hours
Elevation gain: 400 feet
Maps: U.S.G.S. Half Dome

Summary of hike: Mono Meadow is a perpetually wet, marshy meadow fringed with lodgepole pines. The first half mile of the trail steeply descends into the meadow. Downfall logs are used to cross the meandering streams and meadow bogs as you make your way across the meadow. The trail crosses a major tributary of Illilouette Creek and leads to a ridge with a vista point of Mount Starr King, a prominent 9,092-foot dome in the Clark Range. From the granite knoll overlook are also views of North Dome, Basket Dome, Half Dome and Clouds Rest.

Driving directions: From the west end of Yosemite Valley, drive 9 miles south on Wawona Road/Highway 41 to Glacier Point Road. Turn left (east) and continue 10.3 miles to the posted parking area on the right.

Hiking directions: Take the signed trail north, and traverse the east-facing slope past a grove of mature red firs. Descend 250 feet through the forest in less than a half mile. From here, the rest of the hike is fairly level. Cross a tributary stream of Illilouette Creek and meander into Mono Meadow, a small, undisturbed meadow. A stream flows through the flat meadow, making the area swampy. Cross through the marshy parts of the meadow on downfall logs. After crossing, pick up the dry trail on the east end of the meadow. Continue through the shady red and white fir forest on a low divide to a fork of Illilouette Creek, tumbling through a rocky gorge with cascades and waterfalls. Carefully cross logs over the creek, and wind through the nearly flat forest. A half mile beyond the creek is an unmarked clearing on a knoll, just before the trail steeply descends. Leave the trail to the left, and cross the clearing to the plainly visible polished granite slab for the best panoramas. This is our turnaround spot.

To hike further, the trail descends from the overlook and connects with the Panorama Trail above Illilouette Fall, 4 miles ahead (Hike 48).

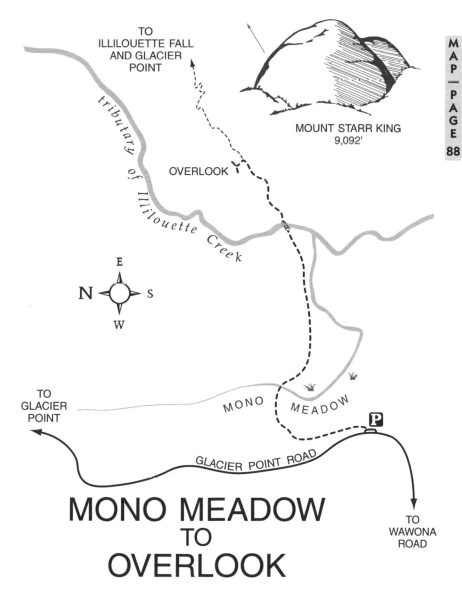

TO
ILLILOUETTE FALL
AND GLACIER
POINT

tributary of Illilouette Creek

MOUNT STARR KING
9,092'

OVERLOOK

N - E - S - W

TO
GLACIER
POINT

MONO MEADOW

P

GLACIER POINT ROAD

MONO MEADOW
TO
OVERLOOK

TO
WAWONA
ROAD

Hike 43
Taft Point and The Fissures

Hiking distance: 2.2 miles round trip
Hiking time: 1.5 hours
Elevation gain: 250 feet
Maps: U.S.G.S. Half Dome

Summary of hike: Taft Point is a rocky knoll that overhangs the south rim of Yosemite Valley from 3,500 feet above (back cover photo). The Fissures on Profile Cliff are five fractures in the overhanging cliff, creating crevasses in the huge granite masses hundreds of feet deep. These deep and narrow chasms and Taft Point are absolutely stunning. This area has truly spectacular views of Yosemite Valley, including El Capitan, Three Brothers and Yosemite Falls.

Driving directions: From the west end of Yosemite Valley, drive 9 miles south on Wawona Road/Highway 41 to Glacier Point Road. Turn left (east) and continue 13.4 miles to the trailhead parking lot on the left side of the road.

Hiking directions: From the parking lot, the trail heads northwest to a trail junction 150 feet ahead. Take the trail to the left. Taft Point is 1.1 mile ahead. (To the right is Sentinel Dome, Hike 44.) A short distance from the junction is a beautiful white quartz outcropping. The trail descends and crosses Sentinel Creek, the source of Sentinel Fall. Continue through a coniferous forest to a junction 0.6 miles from the trailhead. Take the left trail through a shady, lush meadow. (The Pohono Trail to the right leads to Sentinel Dome and Glacier Point, Hike 45.) Weave through the forest past large boulders. Descend to a grand vista of Yosemite Valley, and walk down rock steps to The Fissures. There are no railings—*use extreme caution.* After peering down The Fissures and the 3,000-foot ledge, climb up the angular rock to the railing at the tip of Taft Point. From this open, elevated perch, choose your own route. This is an amazing and unique area to explore. Return along the same trail.

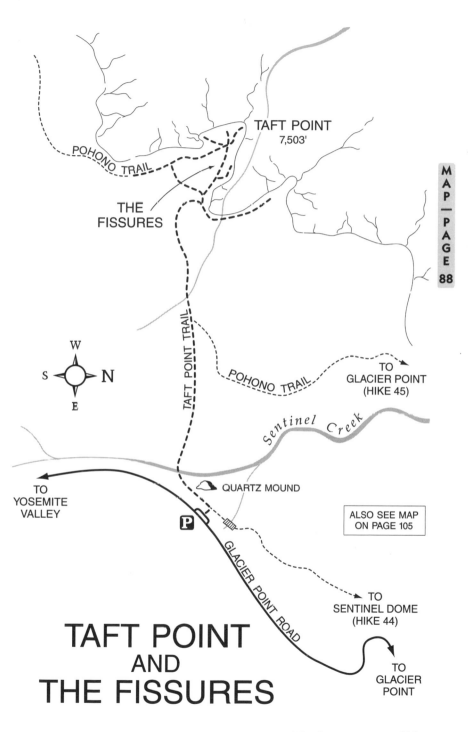

TAFT POINT
7,503'

POHONO TRAIL

THE
FISSURES

W
N
S
E

TAFT POINT TRAIL

POHONO TRAIL

TO
GLACIER POINT
(HIKE 45)

Sentinel Creek

TO
YOSEMITE
VALLEY

QUARTZ MOUND

P

ALSO SEE MAP
ON PAGE 105

GLACIER POINT ROAD

TO
SENTINEL DOME
(HIKE 44)

TAFT POINT
AND
THE FISSURES

TO
GLACIER
POINT

Hike 44
Sentinel Dome

Hiking distance: 2.4 miles round trip
Hiking time: 1.5 hours
Elevation gain: 400 feet
Maps: U.S.G.S. Half Dome

Summary of hike: Sentinel Dome offers one of the highest views of Yosemite Valley, second only to Half Dome. Sitting at 8,122 feet and 4,000 feet above the valley floor, Sentinel Dome has a sweeping 360-degree view of Nevada Fall, Liberty Cap, Half Dome, Clouds Rest, Cathedral Rocks, Yosemite Falls, El Capitan and the surrounding mountain ranges. The unobstructed views are breathtaking in every direction.

Driving directions: From the west end of Yosemite Valley, drive 9 miles south on Wawona Road/Highway 41 to Glacier Point Road. Turn left (east) and continue 13.4 miles to the trailhead parking lot on the left side of the road.

Hiking directions: From the parking lot, the trail heads northwest to a trail junction 150 feet ahead. Take the trail to the right, towards Sentinel Dome. (The trail to the left leads to Taft Point, Hike 43.) Cross a stream on a footbridge. Follow the wide sandy path uphill through open stands of evergreens and granite slabs as Sentinel Dome dances in and out of view. As you approach the south base of Sentinel Dome, cairns (man-made rock mounds) guide you across the open granite. The trail merges with an old, abandoned asphalt road. Follow the road around the east side of the dome to the northern flank. This side not only overlooks Yosemite Valley, it has the least demanding slope to the dome top. The trail to the right leads to the Pohono Trail. Turn left and climb up the granite slope, choosing your own route to the summit. Explore the perimeter of the dome for the ever-changing views from the peaks to the valleys. Return along the same route.

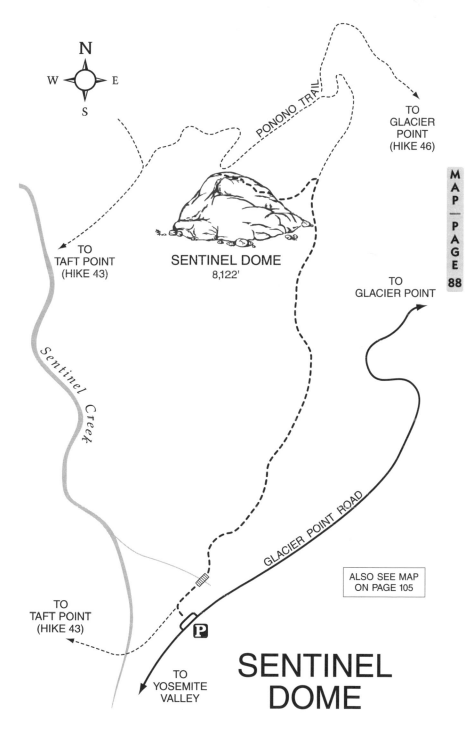

N
W   E
S

PONONO TRAIL

TO
GLACIER
POINT
(HIKE 46)

MAP—PAGE 88

TO
TAFT POINT
(HIKE 43)

SENTINEL DOME
8,122'

TO
GLACIER POINT

Sentinel Creek

GLACIER POINT ROAD

ALSO SEE MAP
ON PAGE 105

TO
TAFT POINT
(HIKE 43)

P

TO
YOSEMITE
VALLEY

SENTINEL DOME

Hike 45
Pohono Trail Loop

Hiking distance: 4.3 mile loop
Hiking time: 2 hours
Elevation gain: 500 feet
Maps: U.S.G.S. Half Dome

Summary of hike: The Pohono Trail is a 13-mile trail that connects Glacier Point with the Wawona Tunnel near the west valley floor. The trail traverses the south rim of Yosemite Valley, passing Sentinel Dome, Taft, Dewey, Crocker, Stanford and Inspiration Points. This loop hike includes the Pohono Trail between Taft Point and Sentinel Dome. The path follows the edge of the 3,000-foot cliffs, with panoramic vistas of Yosemite Valley, Yosemite Falls and El Capitan.

Driving directions: From the west end of Yosemite Valley, drive 9 miles south on Wawona Road/Highway 41 to Glacier Point Road. Turn left (east) and continue 13.4 miles to the signed parking area on the left side of the road.

Hiking directions: Take the trail west (left) towards Taft Point. Walk through an open pine forest, and pass a huge quartz outcropping. Boulder-hop over Sentinel Creek to a posted junction at 0.6 miles. Straight ahead to the west is The Fissures and Taft Point (Hike 43). Take the right fork on the Pohono Trail towards Sentinel Dome. Descend through Jeffrey pine and red fir, and follow the pathway between large boulder outcroppings. Walk through the bucolic forest and through another garden of boulders to the edge of the 3,000-foot cliffs. Follow the edge of the cliffs past magnificent rock formations and vistas. Cross Sentinel Creek to a junction. The left fork is a short detour to an overlook of Yosemite Valley at the edge of the cliffs. The main trail gains elevation between the cliffs and the west slope of Sentinel Dome. A couple of switchbacks lead up to the base of the dome and a trail fork. The left fork leads to Glacier Point (Hike 46). Go to the right, passing a radio tower on the left. Curve around the north side of Sentinel Dome to an old road at a trail fork. The right fork climbs up the dome (Hike 44). Bear left on the old abandoned road along the east end of Sentinel Dome. Follow the wide, sandy path downhill through open stands of evergreens and granite slabs. Cross a stream on a footbridge and return to the trailhead.

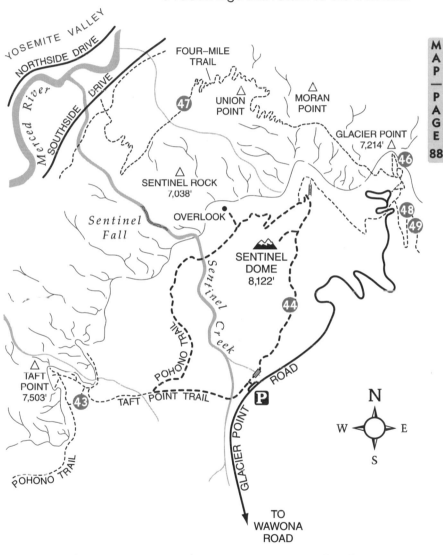

POHONO TRAIL LOOP

Hike 46
Glacier Point

Hiking distance: 0.6 miles round trip
Hiking time: 30 minutes
Elevation gain: Level
Maps: U.S.G.S. Half Dome
Glacier Point Trail map

Summary of hike: Glacier Point is perched on the sheer southern wall of Yosemite Valley at an elevation of 7,214 feet. This short, wheelchair-accessible trail leads to some of the most inspiring vistas you will ever see. Several overhanging platforms provide spectacular views from 3,200 feet above the valley. The eagle's-eye view spreads out in every direction across the valley, highlighted by polished domes, snow-covered peaks, glacially carved valleys, four waterfalls and the vast expanse of the High Sierra. A geology exhibit in an elevated gazebo-like rock enclosure explains the processes that formed the valley.

Driving directions: From the west end of Yosemite Valley, drive 9 miles south on Wawona Road/Highway 41 to Glacier Point Road. Turn left (east) and continue 15.7 miles to the Glacier Point parking lot at the end of the road.

Hiking directions: Take the paved Glacier Point Trail, passing the Panorama and Pohono Trails on the right and concessions on the left. Pass the site of the old Glacier Point Hotel to a magnificent overlook of the High Sierra and Yosemite Valley. A geographic map identifies the many landmark formations, waterfalls, mountain peaks and valleys. From the overlook, bear left to a 3-way split. To the left is the Four-Mile Trail (Hike 47); the center fork leads directly to Glacier Point. Take the right fork to the geology hut in a rock enclosure, with interpretive panels and a reference map of the staggering views. Beyond the exhibit, the path rejoins the main trail. Go to the right towards Glacier Point, passing a connector trail to the Four-

Mile Trail on the left. From the upper terrace, by Overhanging Rock, are views into and across Yosemite Valley. To the right, steps lead down to the lower terrace, with additional views across the east end of the valley.

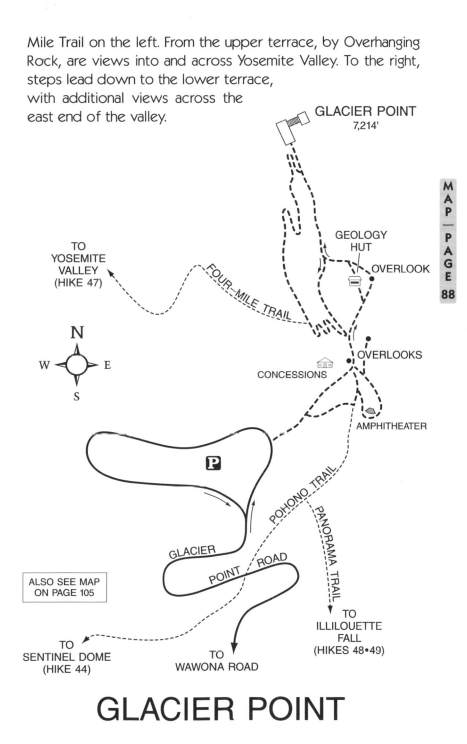

GLACIER POINT
7,214'

M
A
P
—
P
A
G
E
88

GEOLOGY
HUT

TO
YOSEMITE
VALLEY
(HIKE 47)

FOUR-MILE TRAIL

OVERLOOK

N
W ← → E
S

OVERLOOKS

CONCESSIONS

AMPHITHEATER

P

POHONO TRAIL

PANORAMA TRAIL

GLACIER
POINT ROAD

ALSO SEE MAP
ON PAGE 105

TO
ILLILOUETTE
FALL
(HIKES 48•49)

TO
SENTINEL DOME
(HIKE 44)

TO
WAWONA ROAD

GLACIER POINT

Hike 47
Four-Mile Trail

Hiking distance: 4.8 miles one-way to valley floor
Hiking time: 2.5 hours
Elevation loss: 3,200 feet
Maps: U.S.G.S. Half Dome

Summary of hike: The Four-Mile Trail was the original route to Glacier Point before Glacier Point Road was built. The trail was rebuilt in the 1920s and is now 4.8 miles. Our route begins at Glacier Point, overlooking the sculptured landscape of Yosemite Valley. The hike descends 3,200 feet along the south canyon wall via switchbacks to the valley floor. The Four-Mile Trail begins with eastward views towards Little Yosemite Valley, Nevada Fall, Vernal Fall, Liberty Cap, Half Dome and Tenaya Canyon. Along the trail the views open to the west, including Sentinel Rock, Cathedral Rocks, El Capitan, Yosemite Falls, Royal Arches and the Merced River.

Driving directions: Take the shuttle bus from Yosemite Lodge (leaving three times daily) one-way to Glacier Point.

You may also drive, but a shuttle car is needed. Park the shuttle car in the valley on Southside Drive at road marker V18, 1.2 miles west of Yosemite Village. Then, from the west end of Yosemite Valley, drive 9 miles south on Wawona Road/Highway 41 to Glacier Point Road. Turn left (east) and continue 15.7 miles to the Glacier Point parking lot.

Hiking directions: The well-marked trailhead is located at the east end of the parking lot behind the concession building. The trail immediately begins its descent through a sugar pine and white fir forest. There are no trail junctions. Once you begin the descent along the cliff, angling down into the valley, it is a continuous visual treat. Use Sentinel Rock, which is frequently in view, as a gauge to measure your descent. From the base of Sentinel Rock, switchbacks zigzag down the mountain to the valley floor at Southside Drive by Sentinel Beach.

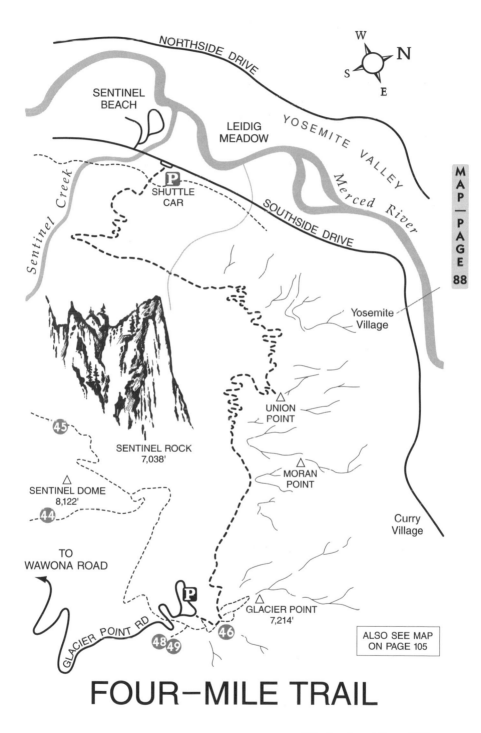

NORTHSIDE DRIVE

W N S E

SENTINEL BEACH

LEIDIG MEADOW

YOSEMITE VALLEY

Merced River

M — A — P — P — A — G — E — 88

P SHUTTLE CAR

SOUTHSIDE DRIVE

Sentinel Creek

Yosemite Village

△ UNION POINT

45

SENTINEL ROCK 7,038'

△ MORAN POINT

△ SENTINEL DOME 8,122'

Curry Village

44

TO WAWONA ROAD

P

△ GLACIER POINT 7,214'

GLACIER POINT RD

48 49

46

ALSO SEE MAP ON PAGE 105

FOUR–MILE TRAIL

Hike 48
Panorama Trail to Illilouette Fall

Hiking distance: 4 miles round trip
Hiking time: 2 hours
Elevation gain: 1,300 feet
Maps: U.S.G.S. Half Dome

Summary of hike: The Panorama Trail begins at Glacier Point on the south rim of Yosemite Valley, passes Illilouette Fall, and continues to the John Muir Trail at Nevada Fall. This hike leads to Illilouette Fall, which drops 370 feet over a granite lip and plummets down the deep vertical rock gorge, crashing onto the rocks below. Above the falls, Illilouette Creek cascades over large flat slabs of granite rock. The Panorama Trail fulfills its name with spectacular bird's-eye views of the entire east side of Yosemite Valley. The stunning geologic features include Nevada, Vernal and Illilouette Falls, North Dome, Basket Dome, Half Dome, Clouds Rest, Mount Broderick and Liberty Cap.

Driving directions: From the west end of Yosemite Valley, drive 9 miles south on Wawona Road/Highway 41 to Glacier Point Road. Turn left (east) and continue 15.7 miles to the Glacier Point parking lot at the end of the road.

Hiking directions: Take the paved Glacier Point Trail 70 yards to the posted Panorama Trail on the right. Bear right and ascend the hill 0.1 mile to a Y-fork. The Pohono Trail bears right to Sentinel Dome and Taft Point (Hikes 44 and 43). Take the Panorama Trail to the left, and follow the cliffside path overlooking Nevada Fall, Vernal Fall and Half Dome. Gradually descend the wooded east slope of Illilouette Ridge on two long, sweeping switchbacks as views open up to Illilouette Gorge and Illilouette Fall. Traverse the mountainside, crossing numerous trickling streams while marveling at the ever-changing landscapes. At the south end of the traverse is a posted junction. The right fork leads 4.3 miles to Mono Meadow (Hike 42). Bear left down a series of switchbacks into Illilouette Gorge.

The thunderous sound of Illilouette Fall can be heard. At the last switchback is an overlook on the left of the waterfall, tucked into the deep gorge. Descend to the raging waters of Illilouette Creek. Follow the creek a hundred yards downstream under the shade of evergreens to an 80-foot metal bridge spanning the creek above the falls. This is our turnaround spot.

To hike further, continue with the next hike down the Panorama Trail. The trail continues to the John Muir Trail and returns to the valley at Happy Isles for a 8.5-mile one-way shuttle hike.

Hike 49
Panorama—John Muir Trail Shuttle

Hiking distance: 8.5 mile one-way shuttle
Hiking time: 4 hours

**map
next page**

Elevation loss: 3,200 feet (gain 750 feet en route)
Maps: U.S.G.S. Half Dome

Summary of hike: This hike is an 8.5-mile one-way shuttle hike that descends 3,200 feet from Glacier Point atop the south rim of Yosemite Valley. The trail ends at Happy Isles on the east end of the valley floor. From Glacier Point, the route traverses down Illilouette Ridge to the top of Illilouette Fall (Hike 48), crosses a bridge over the gorge, and follows along Panorama Cliff to Nevada Fall (Hike 37). The trail joins the John Muir Trail, following the watercourse of the Merced River back to the valley.

Driving directions: Take the shuttle bus from Yosemite Lodge or the Ahwahnee Hotel (leaving three times daily) one-way to Glacier Point.

If you drive, a shuttle car is needed. Follow the driving directions to Hike 46. Park the shuttle car in the valley at the Curry Village parking lot.

Hiking directions: Follow the hiking directions of Hike 48 to the bridge spanning Illilouette Creek just above Illilouette Fall. Cross the bridge and curve left on the Panorama Trail.

Switchbacks zigzag up the forested hillside, ascending the west slope to Panorama Point. Notice the observation platforms back at Glacier Point. Continue uphill, gaining 750 feet along the edge of Panorama Cliff while overlooking Yosemite Valley, North Dome, Basket Dome and Royal Arches. The path leaves the edge of the cliff into the forest, and then returns to views of Half Dome, Clouds Rest, Mount Broderick and Liberty Cap. Pass a junction to Ottaway Lake on the right, and begin descending on a series of switchbacks towards Nevada Fall and a T-junction with the John Muir Trail at 5 miles. The right fork leads 0.2 miles to the bridge crossing the Merced River at the brink of Nevada Fall. On this route, return on the Mist Trail along the north side of the river—Hikes 36 and 37 in reverse.

The left fork returns on the John Muir Trail (the return route of Hike 37). One mile downhill from the Panorama Trail junction is a trail fork at Clark Point. To the right, the Clark Trail zigzags down to a T-junction with the Mist Trail from Nevada Fall. From there, the left fork follows the south edge of the Merced River on the Mist Trail, passing Emerald Pool and Vernal Fall to the Vernal Fall Bridge. Back at Clark Point, the left fork stays on the John Muir Trail and descends to the Vernal Fall Bridge, where both routes unite. Cross the bridge and descend 0.8 miles to Happy Isles on the valley floor. Every route is downhill and filled with magnificent views. Choose your own path.

PANORAMA TRAIL
HIKES 48–49

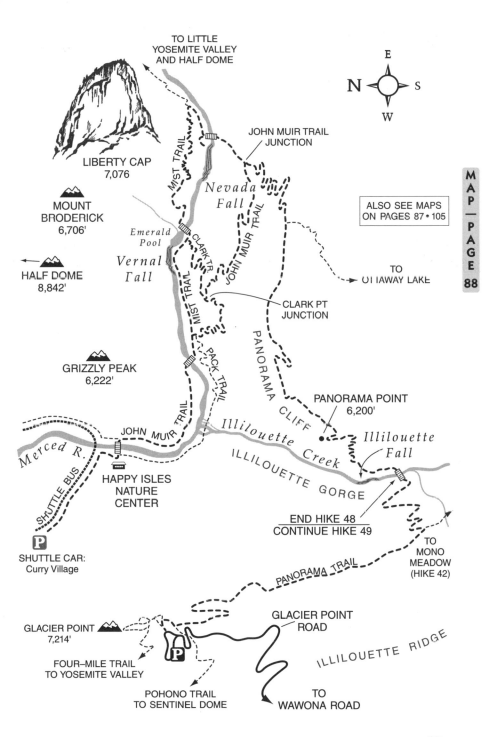

TO LITTLE
YOSEMITE VALLEY
AND HALF DOME

N E S W

ALSO SEE MAPS
ON PAGES 87 • 105

LIBERTY CAP
7,076

MOUNT
BRODERICK
6,706'

HALF DOME
8,842'

GRIZZLY PEAK
6,222'

Nevada Fall

MIST TRAIL

JOHN MUIR TRAIL
JUNCTION

Emerald Pool

CLARK TR.

JOHN MUIR TRAIL

Vernal Fall

MIST TRAIL

PACK TRAIL

TO
OTTAWAY LAKE

CLARK PT
JUNCTION

PANORAMA CLIFF

PANORAMA POINT
6,200'

Illilouette Fall

JOHN MUIR TRAIL

Merced R.

SHUTTLE BUS

HAPPY ISLES
NATURE
CENTER

Illilouette Creek

ILLILOUETTE GORGE

END HIKE 48
CONTINUE HIKE 49

P

SHUTTLE CAR:
Curry Village

TO
MONO
MEADOW
(HIKE 42)

PANORAMA TRAIL

GLACIER POINT
7,214'

P

GLACIER POINT
ROAD

ILLILOUETTE RIDGE

FOUR–MILE TRAIL
TO YOSEMITE VALLEY

POHONO TRAIL
TO SENTINEL DOME

TO
WAWONA ROAD

Hike 50
Lower Chilnualna Falls

Hiking distance: 1 mile loop
Hiking time: 30 minutes
Elevation gain: 300 feet
Maps: U.S.G.S. Wawona

Summary of hike: Lower Chilnualna Falls is a multi-tiered 25-foot cataract that roars through a narrow granite canyon with a tremendous volume of water. The trail parallels Chilnualna Creek along a furious whitewater cascade tumbling over room-sized boulders. Sit and watch the magnificent water display from the surrounding granite slabs and boulders.

Driving directions: From the Wawona Hotel at the south end of the park, take Wawona Road/Highway 41 a quarter mile north to Chilnualna Falls Road. It is located on the north side of the bridge that crosses the South Fork Merced River. Turn right and follow Chilnualna Falls Road 1.7 miles to the signed trailhead parking area on the right.

Hiking directions: Walk up the paved road 0.1 mile to a posted road fork. Bear left ten yards to a second trail fork. The left fork is the stock route to Chilnualna Falls (Hike 51). Curve right on the footpath, and climb the hillside along the thunderous cascades of Chilnualna Creek. A steep path descends to the creek through a forest of redwoods, oak and ponderosa pine. A short distance ahead is an overlook of Lower Chilnualna Falls. Climb granite stairsteps along the raging watercourse, marveling at the powerful water display. A short spur trail continues to a meeting of the rock cliffs and the creek. Return to the main trail, and climb away from the creek up the oak covered hillside, reaching a junction with the stock route on the left. Go to the right on the Chilnualna Falls Trail. Weave through the forest with vistas of Wawona Valley, Turner Ridge and Mount Savage. At the trail fork, the right fork continues on the Chilnualna Falls Trail (Hike 51). Take the unpaved road to the left, which becomes Larke Street, and head downhill through the east edge of North Wawona to Chilnualna Falls Road. Bear left, returning to the parking area.

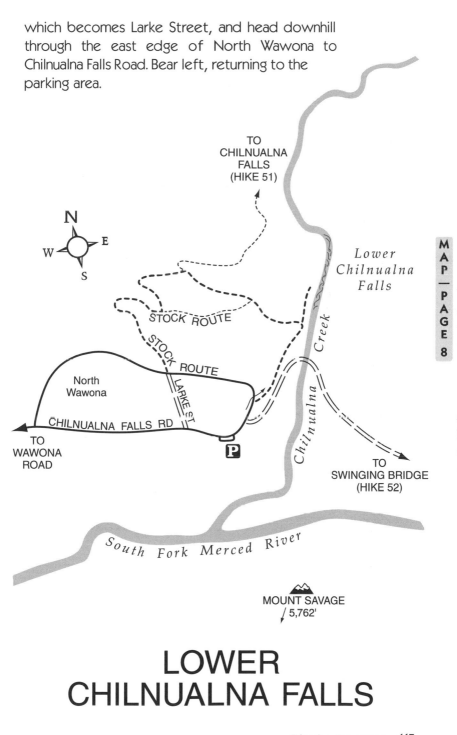

LOWER CHILNUALNA FALLS

Hike 51
Chilnualna Falls

Hiking distance: 8.2 miles round trip
Hiking time: 4.5 hours
Elevation gain: 2,400 feet
Maps: U.S.G.S. Wawona and Mariposa Falls

Summary of hike: Chilnualna Falls twists through a narrow rock chasm and freefalls 240 feet down a narrow gorge from high above the Wawona basin. Above the main falls, a cataract tumbles 60 feet in a series of cascades separated by pools and large granite slabs. This trail heads up switchbacks that steadily climb to the top of the falls, gaining 2,400 feet in four miles. At the top, granite steps follow the creek past the numerous pools and cascades. Along the trail are magnificent views of the forested Wawona area and the Chowchilla Mountains.

Driving directions: Same as Lower Chilnualna Falls, Hike 50.

Hiking directions: Walk up the paved road 0.1 mile to a posted road fork. Bear left ten yards to a second trail fork. The left fork is the stock route. The right fork follows Chilnualna Creek past Lower Chilnualna Falls (Hike 50). Take either route, as both routes merge ahead. Continue uphill on the Chilnualna Falls Trail through an oak, pine and incense cedar forest, entering the Yosemite Wilderness. Curving east, the trail reaches Chilnualna Creek and briefly parallels it up canyon. Curve away from the creek, and ascend a series of long, wide switchbacks, crossing small seasonal streams while the undergrowth changes to manzanita, deer brush and bear clover. The views alternate between vistas of the Wawona Valley and the Chowchilla Mountains to the west and Wawona Dome to the east. At two miles, the trail reaches a granite plateau with an overlook of the tree-filled canyon and Wawona Dome, towering over the valley directly to the east. A half mile beyond the overlook is the first view of a section of the tumbling waterfall high up on the canyon wall. The switchbacks continue uphill, providing more views of the cataract's length. At 3 miles rock hop over a small stream, and enter a forest of incense cedar and sugar pine. Cross a gully and traverse the face of a cliff on a near-level ledge overlooking the freefalling lower end of Chilnualna Falls. From the brink of the falls, a granite stair path follows the creek past a series of cascades connected by pools, where there are great spots to rest and enjoy the creek. At the uppermost cascade is a posted junction. This is our turnaround spot.

TO
BRIDALVEIL CREEK
AND BUENA VISTA
PEAK

MAP — PAGE 8

Chilnualnu Falls

WAWONA
DOME
6,897'

N
W E
S

Chilnualna Creek

Lower Chilnualna Falls
(HIKE 50)

WILDERNESS BOUNDARY

STOCK

North
Wawona

P

CHILNUALNA FALLS RD

South Fork Merced River

TO
WAWONA
ROAD

CHILNUALNA FALLS

Hike 52
Swinging Bridge Trail

Hiking distance: 0.6 miles round trip or 4 mile loop
Hiking time: 30 minutes or 2 hours
Elevation gain: Level
Maps: U.S.G.S. Wawona and Mariposa Grove

Summary of hike: The swinging bridge is a wooden plank and cable bridge mounted on granite rock that spans the South Fork Merced River. A trail parallels the north and south banks of the river along whitewater cascades. The hike can be enjoyed as a short stroll to the bridge or as a four-mile loop. The loop connects Forest Drive with Chilnualna Falls Road, recrossing the river on a covered bridge by the Pioneer History Center.

Driving directions: From Wawona Hotel at the south end of the park, take Wawona Road/Highway 41 north 0.1 mile to Forest Drive, just before crossing the bridge over the South Fork Merced River. Turn right and continue 1.8 miles to a road fork by a rock wall and Camp Wawona. Curve left on the unpaved road, and drive a quarter mile to the signed trailhead at a trail gate. Park in the area on the left.

Hiking directions: Walk past the trailhead gate, and follow the unpaved forest road east. The road parallels the South Fork Merced River upstream. A side path on the left leads down to the river by flat, granite slabs and slow, circling eddies. From the river, the swinging bridge can be seen upstream. Return to the main trail and continue upstream to the bridge. Cross the swinging bridge to the north banks of the river. The path, a dirt road, heads downstream and curves away from the riverbank. The dirt road becomes Chilnualna Falls Road by the trailhead for Chilnualna Falls (Hikes 50 and 51). Retrace your steps for a 0.6-mile round trip hike.

To complete a 4-mile loop, follow Chilnualna Falls Road west through the small town of North Wawona to the horse stables and Pioneer History Center on the left. Cross the covered bridge spanning the South Fork Merced River, returning to Forest Drive. Bear left and complete the loop on the road back to the parking area.

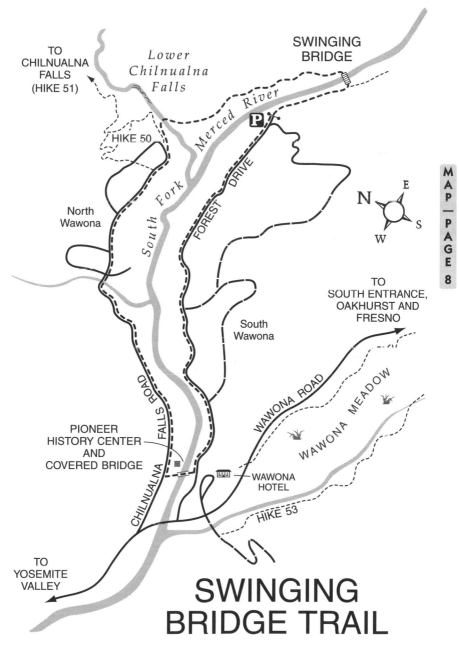

SWINGING
BRIDGE TRAIL

Hike 53
Wawona Meadow Loop

Hiking distance: 3.5 mile loop
Hiking time: 2 hours
Elevation gain: 200 feet
Maps: U.S.G.S. Wawona

Summary of hike: The Wawona Hotel is a beautiful Victorian complex originally constructed in 1876. It now comprises six stately buildings with wide porches and is surrounded by expansive green lawns. Wawona Meadow, a pastoral meadow rimmed with ponderosa pine, oak and cedar, sits in the Wawona basin across the road from the hotel. This hike follows an old road that circles the edge of the meadow along the base of Mount Savage. At the lower west end of the meadow is the well-groomed Wawona Golf Course, dating back to 1917. At this low 4,000-foot elevation, the meadow loop can be hiked year-round.

Driving directions: Park in the lot for the Wawona Hotel at the south end of the park on Wawona Road/Highway 41. The trailhead is directly across the highway from the hotel.

Hiking directions: From the parking lot at the Wawona Hotel, cross Wawona Road to the paved path. Follow the path through the Wawona Golf Course to the posted Meadow Loop. Bear left past the trailhead gate, quickly leaving the golf course behind. Head east along the forested foothills of Mount Savage on the unpaved road. Stroll through the shade of oaks, ponderosa pine and incense cedar while overlooking Wawona Meadow. Cross a fern-lined stream, and follow the south edge of the meadow along the forest floor, parallel to an old split rail fence that once confined grazing cattle and sheep. At the southeast end of the meadow, cross a series of three trickling streams. After the second stream crossing is an unsigned trail on the right that ascends Mount Savage. Rock hop over the third stream and begin the return. Follow the north edge of the meadow to a trail gate by Wawona Road at 3.2 miles. Continue on the footpath parallel to and below the road. The trail crosses to the north side of Wawona Road and returns to the Wawona Hotel.

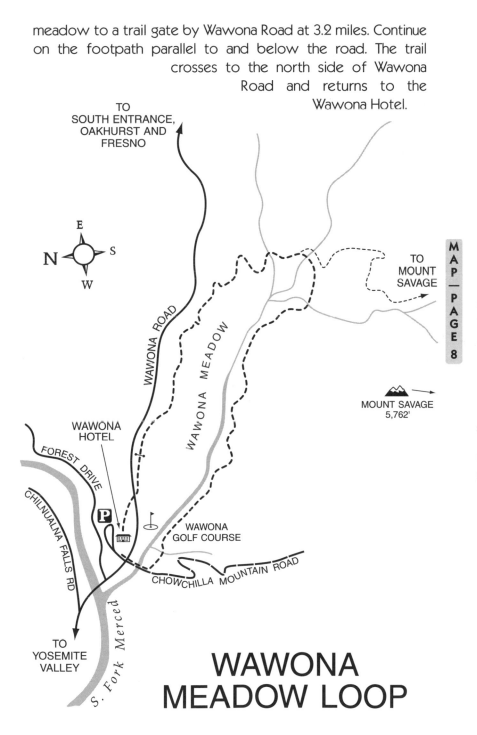

TO
SOUTH ENTRANCE,
OAKHURST AND
FRESNO

E
N — S
W

WAWONA ROAD

WAWONA MEADOW

TO
MOUNT
SAVAGE

MAP — PAGE 8

MOUNT SAVAGE
5,762'

WAWONA
HOTEL

FOREST DRIVE

CHILNUALNA FALLS RD

P

WAWONA
GOLF COURSE

CHOWCHILLA MOUNTAIN ROAD

TO
YOSEMITE
VALLEY

S. Fork Merced

WAWONA
MEADOW LOOP

Hikes 54 and 55
Mariposa Grove of Giant Sequoias

Summary of hike: Yosemite National Park has three giant sequoia groves. Of these three, the Mariposa Grove of Giant Sequoias is the largest and most visited. It is divided into two groves—Upper Grove and Lower Grove. Some of these giant sequoias are believed to be nearly 3,000 years old. Their average height is 250 feet, with a base diameter of 15 to 20 feet and bark two feet thick. Their shallow roots are only 3 to 6 feet deep but extend outwards up to 150 feet to support the massive trees. They are among the oldest and largest living things on earth and are resistant to disease, insects and fire. Mariposa Grove has an impressive display of more than 300 mature giant sequoias within its 250-acre area. One of the largest and oldest trees in this grove is the Grizzly Giant, estimated to be 2,700 years old with a height of 200 feet and a 30-foot diameter. Although the grove is dominated by giant sequoias, there is a forest mix of ponderosa pine, sugar pine, white fir, black oak and incense cedar.

The area has a network of trails that crisscross the grove, allowing a variety of routes. **Hike 54** is through the Lower Grove only. It is 2.2 miles round trip with a 400-foot elevation gain. Information plaques are placed along the trail. The trail visits the Grizzly Giant, California Tunnel Tree, Fallen Monarch and The Bachelor and Three Graces.

Hike 55 takes the tram up to the Mariposa Grove Museum in the Upper Grove. It is a one-way, 2.5-mile trip that descends a thousand feet through both groves back to the parking lot. This trail includes all of the trees in the first hike, plus the Fallen Wawona Tree, Telescope Tree, Columbia Tree, Clothespin Tree and Faithful Couple. The hike also allows a visit to the museum and a quiet walk through the forest. Whichever hike or side trails are chosen, the area is beautiful and rewarding.

Driving and hiking directions for the Mariposa Grove trails are found on pages 124—125.

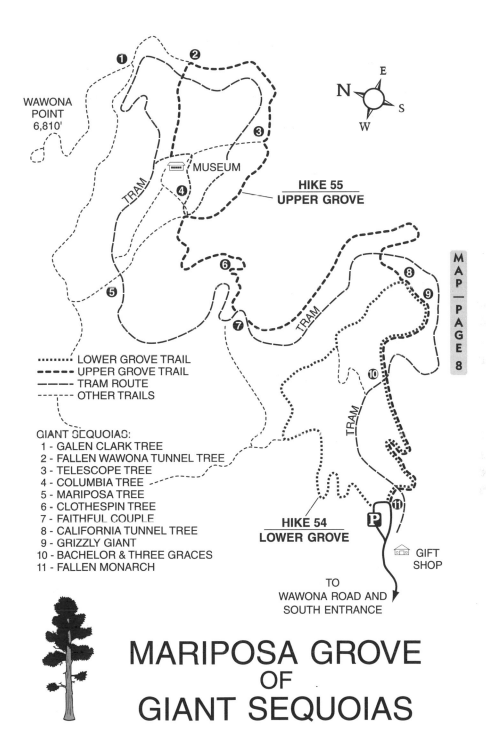

WAWONA
POINT
6,810'

MUSEUM

**HIKE 55
UPPER GROVE**

N E
W S

M
A
P
—
P
A
G
E
8

········· LOWER GROVE TRAIL
– – – – UPPER GROVE TRAIL
——— TRAM ROUTE
– – – – OTHER TRAILS

GIANT SEQUOIAS:
1 - GALEN CLARK TREE
2 - FALLEN WAWONA TUNNEL TREE
3 - TELESCOPE TREE
4 - COLUMBIA TREE
5 - MARIPOSA TREE
6 - CLOTHESPIN TREE
7 - FAITHFUL COUPLE
8 - CALIFORNIA TUNNEL TREE
9 - GRIZZLY GIANT
10 - BACHELOR & THREE GRACES
11 - FALLEN MONARCH

**HIKE 54
LOWER GROVE**

P

GIFT
SHOP

TO
WAWONA ROAD AND
SOUTH ENTRANCE

MARIPOSA GROVE
OF
GIANT SEQUOIAS

Hike 54
Lower Mariposa Grove

Hiking distance: 2.2 mile loop
Hiking time: 1 hour
Elevation gain: 400 feet
Maps: U.S.G.S. Mariposa Grove
       Mariposa Grove of Giant Sequoias—Guide and Map

map
page 123

Driving directions: From the west end of Yosemite Valley, drive 28.5 miles south on Wawona Road/Highway 41 to the Mariposa Grove parking lot, staying to the left at the road fork by the south entrance. The parking lot is 6.8 miles past Wawona. From the south entrance, turn right (east) and drive 2 miles to the Mariposa Grove parking lot at the end of the road. A free shuttle to Mariposa Grove is available from Wawona.

Hiking directions: A map of this hike is found on page 123. The trailhead is at the end of the parking lot next to the inter-pretive display and map dispenser. Take the trail a short dis-tance to the Fallen Monarch tree, which toppled more than 300 years ago. After the Fallen Monarch is a footbridge and the tram road. Cross the road and continue gently uphill on the rock steps to a group of trees called The Bachelor and Three Graces. The Three Graces are grouped together while the Bachelor is off on its own. Again cross the tram road to the trail alongside a stream, and continue to the topped Grizzly Giant, with a cir-cumference more than 100 feet. The trail circles the Grizzly Giant and heads north about 50 yards to the California Tunnel Tree. A tunnel was cut through the tree in 1895 to accommo-date the growing tourist industry. Take the northwest trail that leads to Wawona. At the second junction on the left, head back to the parking lot, completing the loop. (The first junction leads back to The Bachelor and Three Graces.)

Hike 55
Upper and Lower Mariposa Grove
VIA TRAM RIDE TO MARIPOSA GROVE MUSEUM

Hiking distance: 2.5 miles one-way return
Hiking time: 1.5 hours, plus tram ride
Elevation loss: 1,000 feet
Maps: U.S.G.S. Mariposa Grove
Mariposa Grove of Giant Sequoias—Guide and Map

map
page 123

Driving directions: Follow the same driving directions for Lower Mariposa Grove on the previous page.

Hiking directions: A map of this hike is found on page 123. The open-air tram departs from the gift shop near the parking lot every 20 minutes. It winds 2.5 miles through the Lower Grove to the Upper Grove. The drivers stop along the way and share information about the trees and history of the area.

Depart the tram at the Mariposa Grove Museum. After visiting the museum, head east 0.3 miles to the Fallen Wawona Tunnel Tree at 6,600 feet, the high point of the hike. This tree was tunneled out for stage coaches in 1881 and toppled in 1969. Head south along the Outer Loop Trail down to the Telescope Tree, hollowed by fire yet still alive. You may gaze up to the sky through the hollowed trunk of the tree. Continue downhill to Columbia Tree, the tallest tree in the grove at 290 feet. At the nearby four-way junction, take the west trail downhill past Clothespin Tree to the tram road. The road is adjacent to Faithful Couple, two separate trees fused together at their bases. From here, go left along the tram road a short distance, and pick up the trail going to the east, which intersects with the Lower Grove Trail at Grizzly Giant and California Tunnel Tree. Continue west, passing The Bachelor and Three Graces and Fallen Monarch back to the parking lot.

Other Day Hike Guidebooks

These books may be purchased at your local bookstore or
outdoor shop. Or, order them direct from the distributor:

The Globe Pequot Press
246 Goose Lane · P.O. Box 480 · Guilford, CT 06437-0480
www.globe-pequot.com
800-243-0495

Notes

About the Author

For more than a decade, Robert Stone has been writer, photographer, and publisher of Day Hike Books. Robert resides summers in the Rocky Mountains of Montana and winters on the Central Coast of California. This year-round temperate climate enables him to hike throughout the year. When not hiking, Robert is researching, writing and mapping the hikes before returning to the trails. Robert has hiked every trail in the Day Hike Book series. With over twenty hiking guides in the series, he has hiked more than 900 trails throughout the western United States and Hawaii.